Praise for *What You Feel is Real* and Riley's Transformational Coaching

"Not only does my life hold uncanny parallels to Riley's story, but her coaching has given me a sharper focus in achieving both my personal and professional goals. Astoundingly it has helped align my dreams and ready me for my next great steps. Riley's coaching is truly a rewarding and insightful experience."
 – Jacqueline Pierce, Talk Show Host

"Starting in a brand-new direction, like writing and publishing a book, is very intimidating. Riley's coaching helped me focus my attention and gave me the momentum I needed in pulling together my "Let's Get Organized!" book proposal. Now I'm able to take my publishing endeavor to the next level with confidence."
 – Nancy Kalef, Writer and Organizing Consultant

"A few years ago my husband had a heart attack and it scared me to think, 'How very little control we have of our lives.' Since reading, *What You Feel is Real*, it has shown me it's okay to let go and to believe that all things are possible. Even though I already have a thriving business, as my coach, Riley is holding me to task as I further my dream to help the elderly stay physically fit."
 – Colleen Maiorana, President of Maiorana & Partners

"As an employee of a holding company, I help sell off automotive supply companies. What a taxing dilemma. Here I am, doing my job, yet every successful step I take brings me closer to terminating my own position. Riley's coaching helps me keep my sanity and a pulse on my personal and professional options. Although, after reading *What You Feel is Real*, something tells me my work is much greater than me."
 – HR Manager, Big Three Automotive Holding Company

About Riley
The Transformational Coach

Riley has coached hundreds of business executives, writers and creative artists, individuals in transition and seekers of personal growth.

Riley is the mother of three teenagers and lives in Oakland County, Michigan. She is the author of *What You Feel is Real* and its *Dream Journal* companion and a writer of various coaching programs and materials specializing in transformation.

Riley is a Graduate and Lifetime Learning Member of Coach U, Inc. She has a Bachelor of Arts Degree in Communications from Michigan State University.

Her e-mail is **kriley@transformationalleadersintl.com**, and her coaching practice and book's Web site is **www.transformationalleadersintl.com**.

What You
Feel
is Real

An Inspiring Novel of Transformation

KATHLEEN RILEY

Sensible Books
Bloomfield Hills, Michigan
www.sensiblebooks.com

The Library of Congress Control Number: 2006910326

ISBN 0-9761936-1-2

For my son and daughters, Robert John, Jaclyn Renee and Kristen Michele

*"A life filled with purpose is one that
is naturally directed…"*
I say to my children, *"…as it will restore
balance and emotional well-being in your life."*

**In Loving Memory of
My Mother and Father**

The Wisdom of Emotion

In honoring feelings,
You'll discover your wisdom.

In honoring love,
You'll heal your heart.

In honoring truth,
You'll find your soul.

In honoring purpose,
Your well-being will be restored.

In God's love,
We endure.
Amen.

Acknowledgements

When it comes to purposeful-work, there are no rules or standard formulas to reach individual goals or aspirations other than to believe, to commit, to have patience, to persevere, and to listen to your heart when it calls. And so I especially give thanks to all the lovely people who have helped shape my life and support my writing *What You Feel Is Real.*

First, to my children, Robert, Jaclyn and Kristen for providing a constant source of unconditional love and to my late mother, Angeline Riley, for her perpetual source of optimism – I give thanks. To my family, Susan Kerwin, Howard Kerwin, Tom Riley, Jo Jean Riley, Chuck Riley, Christina Riley, and Patricia Riley, for helping me through the many difficult seasons of my life – I give thanks. To Jim Reading, Helen Vardon, Sister Margaret Tierney, Brian Black, Elma Dorty, Tami DeVries, Mary Jo Stevenson, Rabi Swartz, Father Benno Kornely, SJ, Lynn Fink, and Nancy Kalef, for their Judeo-Christian guidance and mentoring; and to Dr. Monvine Saluja for sharing her Eastern wisdom and friendship – I give thanks.

To Dr. Richard Mach and Richard Stocker for their virtues of alternative healing and to Bruce Shlain for his peaceful and loving spirit felt each day – I give thanks.

To Mark Chimsky, Chief Editor, for transforming and
editing *What You Feel Is Real* into novel form, to Paula
Silver, for editing and coaching me through the writing
process, to Eric Zurawski, for his outstanding cover design
and to David Frechette for photographing my picture –
I give thanks. And, a special thanks to Leslie Mangas
for her beautiful design of the *What You Feel is Real
– Dream Journal.*

Finally, to God, for His eternal love that guides my
journey through each new level with grace – I give
thanks. Amen.

Contents

Chapter 1

Dream Journal

It begins in the basement of my home. As I walk down the stairs, I see water flooding the cement floor, about four inches high. They are unclean waters. The water swishes back and forth, hitting the walls as if caused by the pull of a turbulent storm. In the center, I spot the drain.

A woman's voice directs me by saying, "Run for the plunger and work the drain." As I do, the water level lowers; and as soon as it does, shockingly, a woman rises from the drain. It's eerie.

Somehow, I fly up onto a balcony to the far left of my basement room. The woman, who told me to get the plunger, appears and stands close to my right. We both look down at the woman rising from the drain, who casts a glow that lights up the room. She has slightly curly, strawberry-blonde, shoulder-length hair and is dressed in a white gown. She's in enormous pain. As she cries out, she begins to burn up inside. I know she is going to die. I can see the fire's flames when she opens her mouth.

With great inner strength and certainty, the woman next to me whispers, "We need to tell Linda we love her and that it's going to be okay." She adds, "When Linda releases her pain, she will save others." Then she says, "Linda will die."

So, together, we both yell out at the top of our lungs, "We love you, Linda." Linda hears us and cries out with more pain. I can feel her fear of dying.

Chapter 2

My 20's
High Rise Living

Ben and I meet in a bar. Ben has the qualities I want in a man. He is self-made, intelligent and, above all, he appears to have a good heart. It also helps that he is good looking. Put simply, he is gorgeous. Ben takes great care of his body by running and lifting weights at least five times a week. He has dark brown hair and tans a deep, almost black-tone bronze. His sculpted masculine face and shapely feminine lips almost give him an Adonis look. But his eyes lack luster. In fact, his eyes are almost nondescript – and it puzzles me that they are missing a quality, a spark.

We meet during Ben's last year of dental school at a crowded neighborhood pub in San Francisco. By the end of the evening he can hardly stand up straight, yet he manages to remember my phone number and calls the next day for a date. I immediately feel comfortable with him, mostly because he demands little of my emotions. He's easy to be with, as we stay on the surface in conversation.

We share a quirky spiritual connection that has nothing to do with God. We both have encounters with ghosts.

Ben's encounter was with the ghost of his grandmother. When he was a little boy, she appeared at the foot of his bed, dressed in a white flowing gown. Ben thought the woman was his mother checking on him in the middle of the night.

"Mom, why were you in my room last night?" he asked, the next morning.

"No, honey...I wasn't," she answered.

My ghost greets me bedside, but with a slightly different twist. Early on in my relationship with Ben, I'm living with a girlfriend in a two-bedroom Victorian brownstone. The place is so old that we can never hang a picture straight – the floors all sag to the east.

Two weeks before moving with my roommate Jill to the high-rise across the street, it happens to me one night. Looking up, I see a silhouette of a large man. There are no facial features. He is, just simply, a bright glow of neon blue. I don't want to believe what I see. I ignore the image and roll back to sleep. Seconds later, my body levitates some two inches above the bed. A force moves me to the other side of the bed and, not so gently, pushes me against the wall. After my body lowers, I feel the bed's mattress press down next to me – as if somebody is getting in under the covers. That's when I fully awake. I'm scared to death. Obviously, there is nothing – or nobody – there. It doesn't matter. I run as quickly as I can – escaping from my bed to Jill's room.

"Jill, Jill, please wake up!" I whisper in a panic. "I just saw a ghost. Can I sleep with you? Please!" I beg.

"Yeah, yeah, sure," Jill says groggily and hardly waking. I crawl in and share her bed the rest of the night.

No way will I sleep there again. I stay with Ben until

the move.

We have other strange encounters involving my father's spirit.

My father died at the age of fifty-three of an aneurysm. He suffered years, battling alcoholism, and it pained my family to watch him never escape the weary cycle. Ever since his death, I'm certain his essence hangs around – for how long, I'm not sure.

One night, partying again, Ben gets drunk. I mean he is stinking drunk. I've never seen him so bad. He freaks out. Ben stumbles and falls, trying to make it up the stairs to the old apartment building and screams out my father's name, "Jack is here! I can feel him. He's in me." Ben's scary to watch. His drama is so real that I'm convinced the alcohol opened his spirit, to the point that anything could possibly wander in – even Jack's spirit.

Shortly after, my father comes to me in a full-color dream. Or maybe it's more like a nightmare. My father is lying dead in a casket. The room is empty, except for the casket. I walk toward him and slowly lean over to peek inside. He sits up quickly and frightens the hell out of me. He laughs loudly and screams something at the top of his lungs. His face looks evil. The pupils of his eyes are red and the whites are yellow. Eerie. I wake with a sick, sick feeling about him. I remember back to when Grandma Marietta was living. She told me, "When loved ones pass, their spirits visit us in our dreams." My dream and guilty conscience tell me that Jack is upset. He's upset that Ben and I are living together – even though we're engaged.

Living in San Francisco is difficult, especially being away from my family in Chicago while still grieving my father's death. That whole year, I have a dull ache in my stomach and can barely do my job selling ads for the *Neighborhood Voice*, a small newspaper down in the Village.

After unlocking the door and putting the keys back in my purse, I drag my body into the front hallway of our brownstone apartment, feeling ready to collapse.

Ben pops his head in from around the door wall to our bedroom with a letter in his hand.

"I've been asked to join a dental practice in Chicago," he says with a half-smile.

"Really? You're kidding?" I say with a half-smile back.

"No, it's for real," he says. "They'd like me to join this spring."

"That's unbelievable," I say, shocked. "I'm going home!" I wrap my arms around Ben's handsome neck and kiss his beautiful face as tears fill my eyes. The knot in my stomach unravels.

"I have a great idea," Ben says. "Why don't we surprise your mom by wrapping up the letter which confirms my offer and put it in a box to give to her as a Christmas present?" We both giggle in agreement.

Two days before Christmas my mother rests her head on my shoulder, sobbing. I comfort her as best I can. She looks up with streams of mascara running down both checks. "I don't know how I'm going to make it through this holiday," she cries, "I miss your father so much."

I can't take it anymore. To see my mother's withered looks breaks my heart. During better times, mom's a stunningly beautiful woman with dark brown eyes and black wavy hair framing her face and hugging her long elegant neck. She's strikingly Italian and normally possesses a brilliant smile, up until now. I dash to the bedroom – the one that used to be mine – where the present hides. I grab it, rush back to her side and place it in her lap. "Here's an early Christmas present, Mom!" I blurt out. Mom opens the box, reads the letter, and cries again – but this time with joy.

Just then I sense my father's spirit. He's in the room standing off to the far right, in front of the fireplace. I flash to memories of him poking logs in the fire to keep it burning.

"Mom?" I say. "Dad is here right now."

"Yes. He is," Mom replies. "He's here."

Then his spirit moves through my body. I actually feel a tingling vibration pass through my upper torso.

I look at my mother in amazement.

"Did you feel that?" I gasp.

Mom nods yes, unable to speak as my father's energy is still passing through her.

"He's here," I validate once more. "He went through us."

Peace comes over mother's face.

"God answered my prayers," she calmly says. "What more could I ask for this Christmas? You're coming home and your father is with us now"

That night, I crawl under my covers trying to take it all in. I lay there feeling the grandness. Perhaps it's the Universe or God. I'm not sure but it's big. At twenty-three years of age, I wonder about the person I'm to be. Soon I fall fast asleep, soothed by my mother's peace and pleased that my father's spirit has unlocked something mystically wonderful inside.

Level I

Emotional healing is the first form of healing,
and generally deals with hurt feelings we carry
from childhood into our early adult lives.
It's the beginning stage of waking to one's spiritual self.

Chapter 3

10 Years Later
Linda's Basement

When I marry Ben, I know there's a chance he'll be an alcoholic. It's hereditary and he's a heavy drinker. But I love him so much it doesn't matter. I prefer to follow my heart. My father was in his fifties, and his father in his sixties, when 'it' – the alcohol – took their lives. I figure I'll deal with the problem when it comes. But I really think it will be later in our lives – when our children are grown.

You'd think growing up in an alcoholic home, I'd know a lot about the disease. But I don't. My father never made it into re-covery. We lived out in the country, in a place where everyone knows everyone else's business. As a result, we kept everything very quiet – a secret we didn't want out in the community.

There are a lot of alcoholic families that hide. In fact, most times the problem doesn't surface until the disease progresses to the point of destruction. I never went into recovery as the child of an alcoholic. But I now know that everyone in an alcoholic family is sick; therefore, everyone has to go through recovery to heal. Family members are usually codependents, caretakers, or addicts themselves. The good guys want to save the alcoholic. This is what's so sad about alcoholism. Typical-

*ly, when someone is sick, you care for that person. You don't
push them away. You stick by them through thick and thin.
I follow suit, just like my mother who tried to save
my father.*

"Please call Elma and let her know I had the baby," I
say looking up from my hospital bed at Ben with Michelle cuddled in my arms.

"I already spoke to her. She'll be at the house when you
get home," Ben assures me while half in the bag.

*I smell a salami odor coming out from underneath Ben's
clothes. My father smelled like that when he came home from
work at six o'clock every night. The salami smell would breeze
up my nose while I was doing homework at the kitchen table.*

But really, the smell is the stench of ale oozing out of
Ben's body after sucking down four beers at Four Green-
field's Pub next door to Evanston General Hospital.

He's pitiful showing up this way. Luckily, my mother,
bless her heart, is staying with my other two – Billie,
who's five and Lizzie, who's two – until Elma arrives tomorrow. I rest easy knowing they're cared for by her.

Elma enters through the kitchen door with her suitcase
in hand while I feed Michelle in the family room. She
removes her boots, hangs up her winter coat and slips on
a pair of white shoes from a plastic grocery bag. Wearing
a nurse-white top and pants, Elma is a solid-looking black
woman, about five-six, in her early sixties.

The plan is for her to stay ten days straight to give
me enough time to gain strength. Elma takes prides in
showing me a few maternal tricks. "After you bathe her
– rub her down *real* good, like this, with this good smell-
ing powder," she explains. "Now there," Elma says while

wrapping Michelle tight in a towel. "She'll sleep for a good four hours."

At the end of the evening, we prepare six bottles of formula. We line them up front, on the center-shelf in the refrigerator, to make it easy to grab through the night and early morning for Michelle's feedings.

The house is unusually quiet. All three of my children are upstairs asleep and Ben passes out around the same time. Elma and I fold the last few loads of laundry to-gether sitting on the couch in the family room. I enjoy her sweet peaceful energy that seems to come from her center. I can't help but feel it.

"You know, I know things," Elma says rather matter of factly.

"What do you mean?" I ask curiously.

"Well, the doctor told my Momma I was born with a veil over my head."

"What's that?"

"It means that things come to me in my dreams and other times God gives me visions. And my sisters, they don't like me. They're always mad at me."

"You mean they're jealous," I say.

"Ah huh," she says. "And I'm going to tell you some-thing. You better keep an eye on Ben. There's something not right with him. I've been married twice before...both to alcoholics...and one even tried to beat me but I whooped him back."

"You're kidding?" I say amazed by her chutzpah.

But really inside, it's shocking. I can't believe her telling me. I don't dare share my secret. Only my family knows about Ben's drinking and not a soul about the physical threats. Elma's been through what I'm going through and she even

*fought back. My soul opens a tiny bit and God uses Elma
with her sweet energy to coax my frightened child-self out of
the basement. (I call her Linda – she was the one who came
up from the drain, afraid to release the pain.) Linda and I
climb up the staircase and peek around the edge of the broken
wall to listen to Elma's story and then scurry back around
and down-under where it's safe. Quickly my soul closes. I'm
too scared to face the truth. I can't possibly raise three young
children alone.*

We buy a small inboard boat, late summer, and dock
it at a marina north of Evanston on Lake Michigan. It's
a fantastic fall morning with the faint aroma of hickory
carried around by the wind. Ben acts like an eager little
boy as he shouts, "Let's take a ride on the boat today. You
know, it's your birthday present."

"Oh, Ben," I say, "That's not my birthday present. You
know we bought the boat for the family. "I don't want
to take the baby out on the lake with this wind. She's a
mere eight months old. Why don't you take Billie and
Lizzie for a ride in the canal?" I say making a safe suggestion. "I'll stay home." We're only about twenty minutes
from the marina and live in a Victorian brownstone a few
streets west of the lake in Evanston. We've been renovat-
ing it for five years – ever since Billie was born.

It's mid-afternoon. Ben calls me from his cell phone.
"You have to come get us. I fell in the water."

I can hardly hear his voice and his words aren't clear.
"I don't understand," I say. "What about the kids? What
about Billie and Lizzie? Are they okay?"

"They're fine. Please just come get us. Come now," he

pleads as his voice shivers. He sounds terrible. I quickly
load the baby in the car and head north on Main Street.
Immediately, when pulling into the marina, I see Ben
with the kids. Billie and Lizzie are standing on land next
to the boat dock with frightened looks on their little
faces while huddled close to Ben's side. Ben is drenched
from head to toe in his blue jeans and he still has on
his leather coat. The kids aren't wet. They didn't fall in.
Thank God.

In disbelief, I notice Ben's body begins to sway slug-
gishly. Is he drunk? I try to remain calm to make sense of
it all.

"What happened to you?" I ask.

"I was trying to pull the boat into the well. I couldn't
get it in straight because of the wind. The post was too far
off to tie up, so I fell in," Ben says.

"You've been drinking," I say. "I can't believe you're
drunk. How in the world could you be drunk?"

"I stayed up late last night working on the house," Ben
explains. "I only had two beers on the boat."

"That's it for you. No more. Do you hear me? No more!
You put everyone's lives in danger!" The rest of the car
ride and into the evening is dead silent.

*I start to feel guilty. I wonder why I didn't notice. Why
didn't I know he was up late drinking? I can't imagine anyone
in their right mind to be drunk the night before, get up the
next morning, have a couple drinks and be blasted again with
kids on a boat. I could have lost them. I think of the Sigourney
Weaver movie where the alien mother raises her ugly head
to protect her babies. I'm an angry mother. No one threatens
my children. I'm fierce and ugly inside. I store the anger in
the center of my belly – down in Linda's basement where she*

stuffs the black toxins in a furnace bin. His behavior has to
stop. I won't put up with it anymore. Riley rushes up from the
basement and becomes the Miss Fix-It of Ben's disease called
alcoholism. Linda stays behind, managing the anger stuffed
down in the bin.

The fact of the matter is, I can't move fast enough. The
disease is rapidly progressing causing Ben to self-destruct
and take us down with him.

It's a cold and rainy weekend. My family is invited
to watch Billie sing in his first-grade choir at St. Paul's
Episcopal Church followed by a Sunday afternoon soccer
game. But Ben never comes home after work on Friday.
He shares an office only thirty minutes away with two
other dentists west of Lincoln Park. I page him several
times. He never responds.

Still no word Saturday morning. I'm sick to my stomach. I call my mother crying. "Mom, I just don't understand. How could he disappear? It's Billie's first soccer
game tomorrow. How could he? What's happening?" I
call my sister. "He doesn't answer his pager. Should I call
the police?" They're both as baffled as I am.

By Saturday night I'm sobbing with fear – worried that
the father of my children is dead. I sit in my favorite
antique barrel chair in the living room and hold all three
children. My baby sits in my lap – the other two huddle
close to my body. My arms wrap tightly around them
– as if I can possibly protect them from the world that
is theirs. They cry for their daddy and I sob with a deep
wrenching pain in my gut. No Ben.

Luckily, my whole family – my mother, brother, sister,
brother-in-law and sister-in-law – show up on Sunday.
They all know about the trouble with Ben and his dis-

appearance. My brother and sister-in-law play with the kids in the yard in an attempt to distract them. My sister, mother, and brother-in-law console me. We talk of the memories we have about our father's alcoholism. My sister in law, Sandy, comes in from outside. She pulls out an envelope full of brochures that she's picked up at the clinic, where she's working as an intern while she studies for her masters in social work.

"Ben's an alcoholic. You don't have to drink everyday to be an alcoholic...there is such a thing as weekend bingers," she says. "Look...here's the literature from the clinic."

It's too overwhelming for me. I stare at the literature and all my memories come back. Abandonment was something my father used to pull every holiday. He'd pick a reason to have an argument before sitting down for a nice meal and then walk out on us for three or four hours. My mother would pretend nothing happened and the four of us children would go along with her, having our celebration.

Finally, around 6 p.m. on Sunday, Ben calls. He sounds terrible. "I've been drinking," he cries. He's holding himself 'hostage' in a hotel for the weekend.

"Please, please come home," I beg. "We need you. We love you. Please, you need help."

I so desperately need him – more than ever before. It kills me inside. The fear of abandonment is overwhelming. My anxiety rushes in and leaves me in a panic, practically shutting down my whole system. Linda feels the same way with childhood memories flooding up over the surface of her cement basement floor about four inches high. The pain absorbs deeper into every cell of my entire body. The flood practically wipes Linda away.

Level II

*The next level is an inner healing, led by God,
to cleanse the wounds of the heart/soul as well
as the learning of spiritual discernment.
It is a purification stage.
During the cleansing, most people are in intense
emotional pain, causing the heart/soul to crack open
to an awareness of the 'spirit world' and God.*

Chapter 4

Gutting the Main Floor

*With every ounce of energy directed at Ben, my life force is
zapped right out from under me. That's right – I aim to tackle
this beast called alcoholism. I plow right into Ben's circle – to
save him – the same as my mother tried to save my father.
And like those 'women who love too much,' I read everything
possible about the disease. I monitor his every move. I beg him
to stop drinking. I try to control the disease for fear he will die.
I learn a hard lesson. The more you fight, the sicker you get. In
the end, the nasty beast, towering over me ten times, wins. My
health plummets.*

I take a temporary sales position a couple days a week
for a magazine publisher downtown. We share an office
with several other magazines that are part of the same
publishing group.

"I'm not sure what to do anymore. It's really getting
bad," I confide in Larry who works down the hall. Larry
and I started out working together at the college newspaper back in the 70's. Now, Larry is married to Jill and
they're one of our best couple friends.

"He fell in the water with the kids on the boat last
weekend and then disappeared this weekend without

telling us," I whisper to Larry.

"You're kidding. That's awful," Larry says whispering back. "I've seen him after a few drinks at dinner. I knew he was a bit extreme but that's crazy." He scans the bookshelf above his head. Larry pulls out a book called *Codependent No More*, by Melody Beattie and hands it to me.

"What's this book about?" I ask surprised it's on his shelf.

"You'll see...just read it," he says with confidence. "Remember when we lost track of each other for a few years?"

"Yeah."

"Well, I never told you, but when I worked for the *Indianapolis Daily Ledger*, I lived with a woman who was an alcoholic."

"Really...I can't believe you never told me."

"Oh well...you know me," Larry chuckles with his green eyes twinkling behind his skinny, wire-frame glasses. "It was a really bad situation I managed to escape from and I quickly tried to forget about it. Then the next thing I knew, I was living in Chicago." Larry had a habit of hooking up with the wrong kind of women. His carefree personality was like a magnet pulling them in.

"Thanks...I'll read it," I say, noticing that the focus is apparently fixing my behavior instead of fixing the alcoholic.

Later that same week our therapist friend drops by unannounced. Tom's a single guy in his thirties with a tennis build body, blue eyes and black hair. He's been married about three times.

"Last weekend, Ben fell in the water with Billie and

Lizzie on the boat," I say in a panic. "A few days ago he
disappeared and locked himself up in a hotel
room drunk." I compulsively wipe down the kitchen
countertop.

Ben can't hear us talking while he's in back plastering
the ceiling in the family room. Billie and Lizzie are in the
basement watching a tape and Michelle is playing in her
bouncy chair in the kitchen.

"Please tell me Tom...what am I supposed to do? You're
a therapist," I plead. "Please, please tell me."

"You come by my house tomorrow in the day," Tom
says. "I have a book for you."

"Okay," I say.

"You need to get to a support group," he instructs.
"There's one at St. Ives on Monday evenings."

"Okay...I'll check it out."

It feels strange to even think about doing something for my-
self. I'm not the one with the problem. Ben has the problem.
But I have no choice. I'm up against a broken wall. I can't
run the risk of putting my children's lives in danger again.
The book Tom gives me is called The Courage to Change. It's
about famous musicians and movie stars addicted to alcohol
and drugs. They tell their stories of recovery. It's powerful.

Even though it's plain to see Ben is like those people in the
book, it's hard for me to comprehend on an emotional level.
By taking the 'Are you Alcoholic?' test in the back of the book
(as if I'm Ben), the results are proof he is one. Finally, my
intellect outweighs Linda's fears of exposing Ben – I've broken
through her emotional denial.

Then I start to read the book Larry gave me. It's a little
harder because the book suggests changes in 'my' behavior. I
have to shift my thinking and my attitude. I wasn't expecting

*to be the one to do the work. I'm not ready. I have to put
the book down.*

At St. Ives, the crowd is rough and so are their stories.
I feel like I don't belong. They sound weird to me. It's a
different language.

"We have a couple of newcomers tonight. Let's focus on
the 'First Step' at this table."

"George, would you read the 'First Step'?"

"Okay...yeah...sure."

*We admitted we were powerless over alcohol – that our lives
had become unmanageable.*

"Hi. I'm Betty."

"Hi, Betty," the group says together.

"Yeah...well, where do I start? You know, my significant
other... he didn't come home last night..." says Betty
wearing an old tee shirt and pants showing her under-
wear lines. "So I have to give it to my Higher Power...
that's about it for me."

"Hi. I'm Teresa."

"Hi, Teresa."

"Thanks. It's good to be here. I'm just taking it one day
at a time...that's all I can do," Teresa says staring trance-
like at her feet. She's in her early fifties, with curly gray
hair, two front teeth overlapping, and her clothes smell
like cigarettes. "I have to trust that my Higher Power
knows...I just have to turn it over. Thanks for letting me
share. Thanks, I needed to be here tonight."

I'm next as they go around the table. There's no way
I'm going to talk. These people are far worse than me.

"I pass," I say while thinking I'm not like this and neither is Ben. I don't fit in here.

But really, it's hitting me too close. Linda, the child who grew up in an alcoholic home, can't share. She can't talk about the abandonment.

There's nothing wrong with the mix of people; they're family members, just like my mother, my sister, my two brothers and me, affected by the disease. Alcoholism has nothing to do with social status. It's a disease that crosses all walks of life. No matter who we are, we're all the same. The only way to get beyond the disease is to "turn our will and our lives over to the care of God." Once a family makes that shift in behavior and attitude, the alcoholic will change.

We end the meeting holding hands and saying the, "Our Father, who art in Heaven Hallowed be Thy name..."

"Something is terribly wrong with me...I'm losing my hair," I tell Karen by cell phone, heading to the office in morning traffic on the Eisenhower.

"That's not right," says Karen, my old roommate from college. "You shouldn't be losing hair. Your baby is over a year old."

"Clumps keep falling out in the shower," I say flashing back to an image of myself swiping the hair off the drain cover with a Kleenex. "It was just growing back from losing it after having the baby and now it's falling out again."

"Did you see your doctor?" Karen asks.

"Yes...he says it's stress-related."

"Then you need to go into therapy. Remember all the problems Bill and I were having in our marriage?" she says.

"Yeah," I respond.

"Well, I started seeing a therapist and it's helped a lot."

I never thought about seeing a therapist. I always thought it was for the person with the problem. But, by this time, my collarbones stick out above my chest. My skirts hang on me and my pants are baggy. I look anorexic and am down to 108 pounds. I guess, now, I am the one with the problem. Maybe Karen's right...my worrying about Ben is making me sick.

My sister-in-law Sandy refers me to Diane. She's a psychotherapist with a *'been there, done it,'* attitude, which I relate to best.

"Your hair is falling out because you're working too hard at trying to fix the alcoholic," Diane announces bluntly.

I find it hard to talk so I shake my head up and down to let her know I'm listening.

"You have to put the focus on yourself," she explains.

I'm uncomfortable to think I've been handling everything wrong. I should have read the book Larry gave me.

"You need to take care of yourself. You will have to begin by setting boundaries with the alcoholic in your life. You can't fix him."

I sink lower into the couch cushion.

"You have to protect yourself and your children," she continues. "It's his responsibility to fix himself."

I've been trying to fix Ben for six months, since the boat incident, and nothing has changed. Diane works fast to help me put up new walls that make it safe for me and the kids.

The usual Friday evening routine starts with Ben preparing veal scallopini in Marsala wine. He has his own glass of wine, set off to the side, to sip. Ben gets buzzed sipping from a small glass. I find it peculiar.

"Honey," he says, "Billie and I are running out to the

video store to pick a movie."

I rush to the door before he drives off with our son. "No, you can't take Billie. He's not allowed in the car with you if you're drinking. It's not safe." Surprisingly, Ben doesn't say a word and just leaves.

The following weekend before leaving for a dinner party I say, "I've decided tonight we're driving separately..."

"We're married. Why would we go separately?" Ben snarls.

"Okay...if we go together, and you drink, you can take a cab home."

"I don't understand why you're acting this way," he complains indignantly.

"Because...whenever we go out socially, you get blasted. I'm tired of taking care of everything. You're embarrassing to be around. From now on, you're on your own."

Even though I learn how to make it safe, it doesn't solve my worrying about Ben. The stress of it all continues to take a toll on my health.

A rapid series of illnesses hits – one each week.

A butterfly rash blossoms across my face early one morning. "I want to rule out lupus so we'll have to draw your blood," says my internist.

"You're kidding...lupus? That's serious."

"Some blood counts are positive and others negative," he tells me over the phone. "You'll have to come back for more tests." The second round of tests comes back clear.

Then dizzy spells begin. I see an ear, nose, and throat specialist. "It's a mild case of vertigo," says the specialist. "It goes away on its own."

"Really? There's nothing serious about this? I'm okay?"

Next, a huge boil appears on my face. To the derma-
tologist I go.

"I've never seen anything like this," the doctor says.

"What do you mean?"

"The best I can do is give you two heavy doses of steroids to bring the swelling down."

Finally, I come to a conclusion about my illnesses the
night Ben passes out drunk diagonally across our bed.
Simultaneously, I suffer from excruciating stomach pain
and sink to the bathroom floor. I can't get up. The stress
finds a home in my abdomen. The pain is intense.

"Ben, I need help," I shout. "Please Ben. Wake up. I'm
in pain." This goes on for an hour. The kids never wake
and neither does Ben. He's out cold. Drunk.

*As I wait for the pain to subside, it gives me time to think.
Something clicks. Ben's health is connected to my health. We
are in the cycle of pain together. I can only get better if he gets
better. He can only get better if I get better. The stress of it all
is making me sick – it's cycle-somatic.*

The Serenity Prayer

Oh God, grant me the serenity
To accept the things I cannot change;
Courage to change the things I can;
And wisdom to know the difference.
Living one day at a time;
Enjoying one moment at a time;
Accepting hardships as the pathway to peace;
Taking, as He did, this sinful world
As it is, not as I would have it;
Trusting that He will make all things right
If I surrender to His Will;
That I may be reasonably happy in this life
And supremely happy with Him
Forever in the next.
Amen.

– Reinhold Niebuhr

Chapter 5

Beyond My Reach

"*God damn it*, not another crack in the ceiling," Ben shouts while looking up at his work in the family room.

With Michelle in my arms and Lizzie at my feet, I turn my head quickly to respond to a yell at the back door.

"Anyone home?" shouts Leslie. "Its mocha time...time for our morning brew. Oh, where are you Riley?" Leslie's my neighbor from six houses down. She's a tall lanky gal who wears sunshine bronzer on her face and streaks of gold in her hair. You can't help but love her and her glow.

"I'm in the back with Ben!" I call out. "Come on in."

"Oh, there ya'll are," she says beaming.

Leslie's cheery face turns neutral with caution as she enters the tension-filled room – the one with the crack. I can see she feels 'it' – Ben's negative energy. I can't wait for him to leave for work. I'm ready to share what's going on. I want her to understand the dynamics since she watches my kids.

Finally, this morning I decide to let her in – into my secret chaotic world. I'm so ashamed this problem is in my family again. It's hard to let anyone know outside my small circle of family and friends about the alcoholism. It's taboo. I have to have a reason to tell...it's for the safety of my children. Plus, she's a good friend and I need her emotional support.

"Listen, Leslie," looking down to pause and get up my nerve. "This is embarrassing but it's important you know." I look up and make eye contact while fighting off the shame inside. "Ben's an alcoholic. It's important you know what's going on just in case something happens."

"I sensed something wasn't right," she says. "I've sensed it for a long time."

"Really...what'd you think?"

"I didn't know but I could see the unsettled look on your face. Your eyes darting from side to side," she says. "Your kids, too, they seemed nervous and Billie with his stomachaches."

"Ben keeps getting worse and it making me sick and now Billie," I tell her.

"Don't worry. God is watching over you and your kids. I can feel the Holy Spirit working. I'm here to help you. I love watching your kids. My kids love your kids."

Within months, God sends another secret angel. Elma comes back to help me keep up with the housework and laundry twice a week. She acts like a secret agent overseeing the operation of my household. Elma prays, as she folds laundry in the basement, asking for God's power to cast out those demons from every far corner of my house.

"Darling," she says, "your house was full of them. I heard the back door slam when I prayed that last demon out."

She causes me to raise an eyebrow as I listen to her strong interpretation of the spirit world. Linda doesn't think she's crazy. In fact, hearing Elma does just the opposite. She jogs Linda's memory of her father's spirit. I think back to the night when his spirit moved through me.

"Girl," Elma says. "You know, you were your daddy's heart."

How does she know? She's right...I was my father's heart. I was the baby of the family. The little girl he took everywhere. He hated seeing me grow. Once I went away to college, my father never called or visited. The same thing happened when I graduated and moved to San Francisco.

The kids aren't around to hear me cry. Billie and Lizzie are at school and Michelle is napping. With my head down on the dining room table, I sob.

I feel helpless and hopeless. There's nothing left to help my husband and nothing more to help myself and now it's affecting Billie. My only other choices are to send Ben away or divorce him. I'm not ready for either.

I go to church on Sundays only to practice the motions. I'm a believer but in a superficial way. I mumble prayers under my breath that don't connect through my heart. I feel empty and so alone. Even though, Leslie, Elma and I share the same Christian faith, they have a relationship with God. They're connected. I'm not. I need to connect.

I've tried everything to save Ben and to save myself and yet I still can't get past the struggle. I've come to a point of complete powerlessness over his alcoholism. Like our ceiling that's in need of repair, so are the walls of my heart. I can't do it myself anymore. I must let go. I need God to do the repairs.

Tradition has it that past the age of seven, we're forced to conform to a society that's disconnected from who we really are. The nuns put fear in my heart, teaching me that the only way to get to God was through Jesus. They insisted I had to pray to Jesus first. "But Jesus is God. I don't understand the

*difference," I'd say. I already had a natural connection with
God. So, I kept my relationship a secret and channeled my
prayers direct. Not a soul knew, but my own. I need that back.*

I think, maybe I can talk to a priest. Maybe I can find
someone who is connected in a similar way that I was as
a child. Leslie and Elma connect, but it's too different for
me to understand. I dial the number of the church.

"May I speak to someone who is directly connected to
God?" I ask in a serious tone. "Is there a priest?"

"Oh, you need Deacon Mark," the woman on the
phone chuckles, "For sure...he's connected."

I walk down the small dark hall of the church rectory
and softly tap on the first door to the left. Deacon Mark
opens it and directs me in with his warm smile. He is
much younger than his rugged face reveals, with premature lines framing his forehead and around his eyes. Of
course, my skinny body and thin hair are signs of my
hard life.

My hands and body shake as I tell Deacon Mark my
story. "My husband is an alcoholic. He's a falling down
drunk on the weekends...then he straightens up during
the week to care for his patients. I can't divorce him with
three small children. Besides, I still love him. You know...
my father was alcoholic, too."

"What are you doing for *yourself?*" Mark asks.

"I'm in therapy...learning to set boundaries."

"Have you gone to any support group meetings?"

"Yes, as a matter of fact I went to the Monday night
meeting. I didn't like it. I felt as if I didn't belong."

"We have a special meeting for adult children of alcoholics," Mark says. "Would you like to join us Thursdays

at noon?"

"Well...I'll try."

Mark gives me a hug goodbye at the door. In the past, a hug from a stranger was weird to me, but today it's something I need.

At the opening of the meeting we recite *The Serenity Prayer.*

"The courage to change the things I can," we say, "and the wisdom to know the difference."

"Please take a moment of silence for those who are out there still suffering," the leader requests.

I hear the answers to my questions as each person takes their turn talking around the table. There's no cross talk. When it's my turn, it's good to talk without interruption. Finally, my voice is heard by others who understand. There's no fear of ridicule. They help Linda chip away at her imaginary imprisoned walls. Now, the illusion of fear is defused. I feel connected to God inside.

"My sister and I wanted my mother to leave my father. She wouldn't do it. Shortly after our trying to persuade her, an aneurysm went to his brain. He died three weeks later," I say in anger. I immediately weaken as I shift my thoughts to Ben. "I'm afraid Ben will die." Sherry, sitting to my right, hands me a box of Kleenex, as I cry. "They say, we can help the alcoholic to improve if we keep the focus on ourselves," I whimper while blowing my nose and wiping my eyes. "So, I've joined the health club and I'm taking a finance class at night. I'm feeling better about myself. Thank you...I'll pass."

"Thanks Riley," the group says in unison.

At the end, we hold hands and say the *"Our Father."*

"It works...keep coming back," we say together and then everyone hugs.

"I don't understand why you go to those meetings?" Ben mutters out of the corner of his mouth.

"It's for adult children of alcoholics," I say. "The meetings are helping me work on some of my issues with my father."

"Is that right?" Ben says curiously. "I remember when my father went into recovery; my sister and brother went to meetings. I never did. Instead, I left for college that year. I'd like to talk to this Deacon Mark. Do you think he'd mind if I called him?"

"Not at all," I say. "In fact, he goes to the adult child meetings and is a recovering alcoholic himself. But please don't tell him I told you that."

I remain cool as I hand him the phone number. I don't want to jinx his revelation. The voices inside my head shout out, "It works...keep coming back."

A Morning Prayer

Help me, dear Lord, to live through this day
as You would wish me to.
And if I fail, then please forgive the
wrong things that I do.
Give me the strength to comfort those
who need a helping hand.
Give me a loving heart that I may better understand.
Help me to solve the problems
that are sure to come my way
But not forget the blessings that
are part of every day.
And finally, Lord, walk with me.
My faltering footsteps guide for
I may never be afraid
if you are by my side.

– Anonymous

Chapter 6

Workmen Arrive

My mother walks in the kitchen door with three boxes of animal cookies and silly toys from the dollar store. She holds my two youngest – both small enough to put in her arms – hugging and kissing their sweet faces. She runs them to the toilet and wipes their bottoms and runny noses, while I get dinner ready. I put a fresh pot of coffee on. We fill our cups and shift the conversation to the dining room table.

"So what's going on?" she asks.

"I think Ben is blacking out," I whisper. "His over-coat and wallet were missing. He says they were stolen from his health club a few days ago. He isn't sure. I left the house to run over to the preschool. I left the back door unlocked. I was only gone ten minutes. When I came back I found Ben's coat wrapped in a fresh plastic cleaner's bag hanging in the hallway closet. In the dining room I found his wallet sitting on the credenza."

"You're kidding," my mother says as she shakes her head. "How in the world?"

I tap her hand to get her attention to hear more while I continue to whisper. "Listen, Mom. So, I say to Ben, 'You won't believe it but your coat and wallet showed up.' He says, 'What do you mean?' I tell him what I told you and he acts miffed. Then he says something stupid like, 'It must be my father's ghost that returned them.' Either he's going crazy, blacking out, or another woman is in the picture."

"He must be blacking out," my mother says. "Here's a little prayer that will help you through," Mom says handing me a small card. "It's such a nice prayer. I laminated several copies and I've been handing them out to everyone. It's called *A Morning Prayer.*"

"I could use a new prayer," I say glancing down as I read, '*Help me to solve the problems that are sure to come my way but not forget the blessings that are part of every day.*' This is nice...yeah, this is nice...thanks," and then I kiss her cheek. I place the prayer up on the side of my refrigerator, held by a magnet and make it part of my routine several times a day while loading the dishwasher.

Ben turns stiff while he drinks. He falls asleep either standing up or sitting in a chair, passed out with a cigarette that doesn't quite make it to the ashtray.
He's a hazard.

Waiting for something to happen is a ridiculous thought – because it's happening now. The house could burn down and we'd all be dead.

Eyes fixed on the prayer, up on the refrigerator, I mumble the last two lines, "...And finally, Lord, walk with me, my faltering footsteps guide for I may never be afraid if you are by my side."

I start to take little steps.

"Ben goes to twelve step meetings and sees a therapist, but it's not working," I explain in a panic to my sister-in-law Sandy over the phone. "He's goes stiff when he drinks and leaves cigarettes burning on the cooktop. Last weekend, he fell off the deck on our friend's yacht and the weekend before last, his friends carried him out of the pool hall. He literally passed out over a pool table."

"The disease is progressing quickly," explains Sandy. "You need an intervention."

"How do I do that?" I ask.

"Call Dr. Stewart. He's an intervention specialist and he can organize everything."

A committee starts up in my mind. Can I really do this? His partner will find out. Where will they send him? How will I take care of the kids by myself? Who will pay the bills?

"There's a rehab center in Atlanta," Dr. Stewart says in a fatherly soft voice. "They specialize with people in the medical field."

"Really? How long is the program?" I ask.

"This one is longer, it's thirteen weeks."

"Thirteen weeks?" I feel a lump push up in my throat. "How much does it cost?"

"You'll have to call and ask," Dr. Stewart suggests. "Sometimes insurance will cover it."

The lump shuts off my breathing. I panic. Suddenly, my baby steps feel a little too big. I can't go any further.

It's Saturday night. We dress up to go to a dinner party at Steve's home. Peculiar behavior, again – I notice Ben locks the bathroom door as he showers and shaves. When he's ready, Ben looks incredibly handsome and appears in a great mood as we kiss the kids goodbye. I can't help but notice this *electrifying* energy that gushes out of him, especially when he's in an inebriated state. Admittedly, it holds some kind of seductive power that confuses both the children and me when we're not on to him.

"Can I mix you a drink?" Ben's partner asks.

"Sure...a bourbon-on-the-rocks," Ben says with a silly grin sliding off his shapely lips.

My committee starts again. Maybe it'll come out tonight. Maybe Steve will see the problem. Maybe he'll see Ben is a falling-down drunk.

Oh my God, another couple has arrived for dinner. I hear them knocking at the back door. It's a doctor and his ex-wife who both live in the neighborhood. Fear sets in. Now, no one can know. This can't get out in the community.

Ben recites his favorite *Saturday Night Live* skit once everyone settles around the dinner table. He starts telling it over again, a second time, not realizing he already told it. Joanne and I exchange a look, knowing we're the only ones to notice. The others aren't even listening, as they are too busy talking amongst themselves.

"Ben?" Joanne calls out. "Would you help me carve the tenderloin in the kitchen?"

"Sure thing...that's my expertise," Ben slurs, swaying his way into the kitchen.

Next, I excuse myself from the table and rush into the kitchen.

"Lets get him to lay down somewhere," I suggest, "before he passes out."

"How about upstairs in our spare bedroom," Joanne responds. Then she steadies him up the staircase.

"Ben's not feeling well," Joanne says daintily returning in her seat. "He'll join us later...go ahead, lets eat." No one seems to mind and shortly after the main course the other couple announces they have to leave. There's some kind of emergency at home they don't wish to share about their daughter.

Now, I'm face-to-face with Steve standing in the kitchen. Here's my opportunity to open up.

"Steve," I say trembling inside. "Ben has a problem... Ben's...well...Ben's an alcoholic."

"No? You're kidding?"

"He's been this way for awhile," I say apologetically. "I didn't know what to do...I didn't know what to say. For the longest time, I didn't know what to say."

"I love Ben...I love him like a son. What can I do to help?"

"I want to send him away to a recovery program. I've done the research."

"Whatever you think is best. I'll do whatever you need me to do."

"I found a program in Atlanta. We have to intervene and send him away...he's very sick."

By this time, Ben wakes up and comes back downstairs looking dazed and confused.

"Come on Ben...lets go home," I say. "Thanks, Steve and Joanne...we'll talk later."

Finally – two long years of silence is broken. I can't believe it's happening. My imaginary committee proudly cheers me in the background. I'm relieved the secret is out. I feel a tingle of excitement knowing my life is about to change and hopefully for the better.

Oh, how I labored over this day for years and wondered if and when it would ever come. It constantly wore on my mind. I didn't want to be the one to tell his partner. Even though I

*ended up telling, it was Ben who made it obvious to Steve.
I simply verbalized what Ben was showing Steve. I really
should have left Ben a long time ago, but I didn't have the
courage to make the break. Like a lot of young mothers, I
feared that supporting and caring for three small children
alone would be an almost an impossible task. I had no idea of
how we'd all survive yet I had no idea how much damage
I was causing myself by tamping the truth down…way down
in the basement of my soul…where Linda waits to release
the pain.*

I can't even pull my hair back in a ponytail or put it
up because it reveals my bald spots. I have half a head of
hair left and my weight is down to 105 pounds. Again,
the blood tests show I'm fine. The doctor says, "It's stress-
related."

I've taken the summer off with plans to start another
part-time job in September – another fill-in job for a
friend going on medical leave. How ironic. *I* should be
the one taking medical leave. At least a job is security – a
most important *feeling* at this time in my life.

I'm too scared to make the phone call. It's like turning
my husband in to the police. I need a calm setting. I load
the kids in my minivan, strapping the two girls in their
car seats in the middle and buckling Billie safely in the
seat way in the back. I head west on the Eisenhower
to Mom's.

I close the door to her bedroom, grab the phone off her
nightstand and sit on the floor with the phone in my
lap. The closer to the floor, the better…it's all I can do
to ground myself and keep my body from shaking. My
palms feel clammy-cold while I push the buttons.

"Dr. Stewart," I say, "I'm ready to do the intervention. Ben's partner knows."

"Okay, here's the plan...find a place where we can all meet. Gather your family and have Ben's bags packed. Oh...and buy him a one-way ticket...and make sure you designate someone to escort Ben on the plane ride down."

As he finishes explaining, my fears dissipate. The emotional weight gently lifts off my chest. *A Morning Prayer* has been answered.

"Each person will tell Ben how his alcoholism has hurt them, how he disturbed their lives," Dr. Stewart continues.

"I've talked to Steve about meeting at his house. It's all set. Ben thinks he's coming to discuss the office remodeling plans with Steve."

My mother, brother, sister-in-law, sister, brother-in-law, Steve and Joanne, are all there. My mother's boyfriend, Jim, is there too, with a round-trip ticket to escort Ben to Atlanta. Two recovery members from rehab will be at the gate when the plane lands, to take Ben directly to the hospital.

As Ben steps into the den, he has a somewhat pleased look on his face to see us.

But it's not what he thinks.

"Ben...I'd like you to meet Dr. Stewart," I say with caution, in anticipation of a time bomb ready to explode.

The doctor steps forward to shake Ben's hand.

I fade into the background.

"Ben, I'm the liaison from a recovery center in Atlanta," Dr. Stewart states in a cool manner.

I see apprehension and fear blush across Ben's face. *He's made the connection.*

"I knew something was up," Ben says trying to save face. "I knew this was not going to be about the office plans."

"Your family is here to tell you about how they feel about your drinking."

One by one, my family members express their accounts of hurt feelings.

I cringe as I watch his reaction.

"Ben, remember when you were so drunk you urinated in my kitchen sink," says Sandy, my sister-in-law. "That really upset me."

"When we took the boat up to Wilmette and you passed out," says my brother-in-law. "I had to bring the boat in by myself."

"I didn't like it when you kissed and hugged me too tight when we went out for dinner," says my sister.

"When we went skiing at Blue Mountain and you passed out at the Moose Preserve," says my brother. "I had to carry you to the car."

It's my turn. It's hard to focus. I'm nervous. It's overwhelming. Finally, I blurt out a whole series of images that stream from my mind.

"The time you locked yourself in a hotel room and disappeared for the weekend, I thought you were dead. Another time, Michelle cracked her head open, and you didn't think it was a big deal," I cry. "And then when Billie was an infant, you almost crushed his head. You fell asleep in the rocking chair and he rolled out of your arms," I sob. "You've put our children at risk and I'm afraid you're going to die...you're going to die like my father and like yours. Please…you need help. Really!"

"Please, Ben. We love you," my mom says. "Please Ben…you need help." She stares at him in deep sorrow while silence fills the air.

"It's *best* for you," I say, still quivering from my outpouring of emotions.

Standing off to the side, Dr. Stewart gestures with his hand that it's time to take him away.

"Well, it's time," says Jim. "Your plane leaves at seven p.m."

"Yes…it's time," says my brother.

"I can't just go," Ben pleads. "What about my kids? I have to say goodbye."

"No, you have a seven o'clock flight," my brother says firmly.

I hand Ben his bag with enough clothes to last a few weeks.

"What about my patients?" Ben asks.

"No, no. I can handle it," assures Steve. "You have to go."

By this time, he's very angry – mostly with me. Ben walks out as Jim escorts him to the car. They manage to swing by our house to say goodbye to the kids. I stay behind. My body is emotionally raw. All my baby steps just became one giant leap.

Chapter 7

Flood Subsides

"I don't know why you sent me here. I don't need to be in a hospital," Ben spews. "I'm not going through the DT's." He then slams the phone down in my ear.

Each day I visualize a dark mushroom-shaped cloud hovering over the roof of my house that somehow has a hold of my emotions. I struggle to settle my children in bed. The rest of the night I clean, fold laundry, and review finances. Before bed, I step outside on the deck to have a cigarette, cry a few tears, and ponder my life while looking at the moon. That's my routine.

"Where's daddy?" my little girls ask as I tuck them in.

"Daddy is sick and good people are taking care of him," I say. "We'll visit him in a few weeks."

Billie is eight. He understands a little better. "Mommy... Daddy's getting help. He's going to be okay? Right?" he asks.

"Yes, Billie," I answer. "He's doing great. We'll visit him. It will be fun and we can take a tour of the Coca Cola factory that's near where he is staying."

After about three weeks, my kids have a routine. They're in bed by 8:00 p.m. and so is the dog. The sweet aroma of peace nestles in the very center of my stomach and extends out. We are calm and I'm the mother I truly desired to be – fully there.

I work on healing. I begin journaling my thoughts and feelings. Amazingly, my body quickly restores itself by gaining weight and growing back my hair. My face has a more healthy glow. Every glimpse in the mirror makes me marvel. But the unexpected images appearing in my mind's eye hark back to what's still sore and tender inside. The flashbacks are beyond my control. I have an image of Ben chasing me around the dining room table with Billie. I'm fearful Ben will hurt me like before, but this time I have our baby in my arms. The flashback continues. The next morning, I call the abuse hotline number and we meet with a therapist. After that he never lays a hand on me again. Another flashback comes out of nowhere. I see myself begging Ben to come home from a weekend disappearance. I don't know his whereabouts. I need to take Michelle to the hospital emergency. She has croup and can't breathe.

"Can you make it as early as next week for family therapy?" asks Wendy over the phone. She's assigned as our marriage counselor from the rehab. "It would help Ben's recovery to have you there."

"I've been working my recovery for a good three years – seeing a therapist, going to support group meetings, reading self-help books, praying and journaling," I tell Wendy. "You want me to sit and listen to lectures about alcoholism? I can't leave my children that easily."

To my surprise, they put us with three other couples for a group session. I actually like it. I feel safer speaking in front of a group about our problems rather than being alone with Ben.

"I was searching for my cigarettes hidden under the floor in the bathroom cupboard." I explain to the group. "When I found my empty cigarette pack, I discovered Ben's empty beer cans."

"I just don't understand why you need to smoke," he says, averting attention from my discovery of his beer cans. "That's ridiculous."

"Every night, by the end of the night, I'm a wreck," I explain. "I need a break caring for the kids by myself...so I called Tom to see if he'd bring me a cigarette. He dropped one by. Why do you care if I smoke? You smoke when you drink!"

Ben clams up and doesn't respond.

"Oh, I get it. You think I'm having an affair with Tom," I say later that evening.

"Well...yeah I worry. Some of the guys I know – their wives are cheating on them or they're going through a divorce while away," he says. "It's common to see people having affairs with each other during the thirteen-week stay. I know a few guys and gals who got caught sleeping together and got kicked out of the program."

"Are you kidding? Please don't worry about me." I say assuringly, "I've always remained true."

You don't realize you've been stripped from your personal power, until after the fact. It's profound to see myself gain it back while Ben's in rehab. When you're in the cycle of abuse, it's easier to not feel anymore. The abuser weaves a web of bewilderment. Feelings become disoriented. You don't know what's coming next. You lose touch with reality. You don't trust yourself. The only emotion you know is love. You're desperate for love. You want to be loved. You will do anything to

feel love. Sometimes it makes you want to cling to the abuser,
even more so, or to someone else.

My therapist tells me when Ben returns from rehab, it will
be like being married to a new man. It will be a new relation-
ship. I want nothing more than to feel love.

Summer ends, the kids are in school and it's my first
week on the job at *Style Today*. The office overlooks the
Chicago River and Lake Michigan from the far southeast
corner, and splatters of purple, orange and yellow flow-
ers line the park as I peer down from the lobby window.
Working three days a week gives me a nice balance away
from home and a sense of financial security.

"If I seem a bit off focus, it's because my husband
is moving back home," I say to Jenny, my co-worker.
"We've been separated for a few months."

"Don't worry. I understand," she says. "Hopefully everything will go just fine."

"Hi, Riley...welcome aboard...thanks for helping us
out," says Mitchell Gray, the advertising director, over the
phone.

"Thank you...it's so nice to be here. What do you want
to do about the Jillian account? They don't like their
October position."

"Tell them we'll guarantee the first third of the magazine if they commit to another ad in November."

"Great...I'll call them right away."

The following week, Mitchell arrives to help acquaint
me with the magazine. He stares at the pictures on the
wall and then back at me, a few times, as he tucks in his
shirt while I'm on the phone. He's a tall, well-built man,

carrying a scent from afar that seems to stir *Linda* inside. Why does he stare so much? I shrug it off and think it's because I'm tan from my boating weekend on Lake Michigan.

After a couple of weeks into the job, I sense more interest. Mitchell calls back too quickly from strange places, like airplanes and cabs. My questions aren't that important. I know a New York manager's pace.

"I have a feeling this man has a crush on me," I tell Larry, down the hall. "What do I do? This is really awkward."

"Do nothing," he answers. "Just do your job and ignore it."

From a distance, I can see Ben walking slowly across the field to Billie's soccer game. His steps carry a deliberate ease so unlike the old Ben. As he comes closer, we embrace in a loving hug while the game plays on. My hopes are high – he's my new love.

"Ben's going to be in the pink clouds at first," says Wendy. "You know, very peaceful. There's an adjustment period. You can expect it to get rough. You'll have to start marriage counseling right away. I'll explain it to Ben when he joins in on the phone conversation. And remember, Riley, you'll need to report any behavior changes immediately. *You will see a sign of relapse before it happens. You will see it in his eyes. The peace will go away.*"

Ben joins in on the conference call.

"Ben, there is an agreement between you, Riley and the rehab center. I'll need you to both sign it and send it back to me," explains Wendy. "We're asking you to promise to continue with individual counseling, to go to three meetings a week, and to see a marriage counselor."

"Screw them," Ben says as he slams the phone down. "I'm not doing all this,"

I'm shocked by his response. "But we have to…it's important," I plead. "We need the marriage counseling."

"No way – I'm not going. And I'm not doing three meetings a week either."

.

"It was heaven having Ben back…but it only lasted for a brief time," I say to my support group. "Now…the peace is gone. Wendy was right. His eyes do look empty. They lack something – come to think of it, they always have."

My stomach is unusually nervous – nervous about being with Mitchell. He's waiting on the south side of the Hancock Building. I swing around curbside in my grey mini-van. Mitchell's eyes catch mine as he walks to the front of the vehicle before getting in. Hum? Strange feeling. His larger-than-life presence is strong and equal to his stature.

On our way north of the city, we lunch in the DePaul vicinity.

"Here…let me help you with your chair."

"Oh, thank you," I say as Mitchell pushes in my chair. It's like being on a date. Mitchell's nice. He's a gentleman. He asks a million questions.

"So, you used to live in Chicago?"

"Yes…I grew up here," Mitchell says with his eyes growing wider. "In fact, it was a neighborhood just around the corner, not too far from Wrigley Field."

Halfway through, I study his face. He's very nice looking.

His eyes draw me in. They are dark-brown, warm and gentle. A tale opposite the one told in Ben's eyes. Suddenly, without warning, I fall in. A connection occurs. It's as if God reaches through Mitchell and grabs that tiny part inside of me – the part so desperately wanting to be loved. The unclean waters subside and Linda comes up gasping for air – bringing up all of her emotions.

Chapter 8

Hallways & Mirrors

Mitchell dashes through the double doors from the office lobby returning for another Chicago visit a few weeks later. The room is full of clients and magazine sales people, drinking and eating shrimp cocktail and fancy fruits at the company holiday party.

Linda instinctively wants to run. Get a hold of yourself, girl. You have to say 'hello' and tell him when you plan to pick him up in the morning. We have a day of calls together and a luncheon celebration with the staff tomorrow.

Mitchell is standing in the hall talking to a couple of associates. I try to catch his eye to let him know I have something to tell him. He walks closer and puts out his hand to shake mine.

"I guess this is it," he says. "It's been a pleasure working with you."

I take a step back and lean in to shake his hand.

"No, we have calls together tomorrow," I remind him. "We have an 8 a.m. and I'll be by the hotel to pick you up at 7:30."

The next morning, he flies out the front door of the hotel and lands in the cab beside me. He looks a bit crusty.

I can see he blew dry his hair without styling it. *Linda*
loves his boyish look.

"The party ended at a diner with a group of us eating
Coney dogs 'til 2 a.m.," he says and then laughs.

I think he's trouble.

"He's fun," thinks *Linda. "He likes to play."*

On our first sales call, he's great. Not high pressure. He's
personable and his intelligence is evident as he speaks
with the client. When leaving the atrium-complex,
Mitchell wants to check out the vehicle displayed on the
floor. He gets behind the wheel.

"Let's you and I take off together in this car and go to
Florida," he says looking up. Mitchell has no idea how
strongly his words play inside of me. I'd love nothing
better than to run away from the hell that I call my life.

"Oh, wouldn't that be fun," I lightheartedly respond.

Our next call cancels.

"You know, I'm really hungry," says Mitchell. "I could
go for breakfast."

"Me, too," I say.

Mitchell pauses to collect his thoughts. "I'm trying
to figure things out," he awkwardly reveals. "You know
what I mean...what's it all about? Life?"

I kick into recovery talk. "I've been working hard at taking care of myself," I say passionately and then start rat-
tling through my health regimen...diet, exercise, quitting
smoking and practicing personal responsibility.

"Well, I can see your glow," he says staring at my face.
Then Mitchell becomes flustered and completely blanks
out on his train of thought. He's embarrassed. I laugh.
Then we laugh together. It's not that funny, but for some
reason it tickles me inside and turns into uncontrollable

laugher. Tears well up in my eyes.

We pass the health club that Ben and I belong to, and I point it out to Mitchell.

"Ben works out all the time and he's in good shape," I say. "I'm not that perfect and I don't necessarily care about having to be that perfect."

"I play floor hockey with my buddies," says Mitchell.

Then something comes over him. Mitchell's eyes turn downward making him appear modest and uncomfortable at that precise moment. As I glance at him, it's as if an invisible dart, fastened by a strand of love, shoots straight into my heart from his.

At breakfast my energy pulls toward him like a magnetic force. Everything he says seems very interesting even though I know it really isn't. A chemical reaction is altering my body and I feel a seductive power between us. I excuse myself from the table and stumble into the ladies room. I look in the mirror and notice I look high. I can hardly stand up straight.

Get a hold of yourself. Regain your composure. This is not normal, I say, trying to ground Linda's spirit.

It's the end of the day and time to part. I notice it's hard for Mitchell to say goodbye. "If you ever need anything – you call me." Then an idea pops in his head. "Why don't you come to New York? Why don't you come to the Christmas party? We'll fly you in. We'll pay your way," he suggests.

"I would love nothing better than to come to New York but I'm just too busy," I say. "I can't. I have to stay home. I have my kids."

We shake hands and he leaves to catch his plane.

I feel completely drained of energy – as if the life has been sucked out of me – as I drive away. I swing by Leslie's to pick up my kids and tell her everything. That night I lay in bed with my mind racing. I review word-for-word every spoken sentence with Mitchell and re-live every intense pleasurable feeling that day. I can't make sense of anything. I float through the next two days with my body turned inside out. This is crazy. Linda is going wild inside – like an animal trapped inside a cage. I'm trying to keep her down. I'm damned if I do and damned if I don't. I can't possibly have an affair. Can I? Just the thought of one sends me reeling, yet the draw is so powerful.

By Sunday evening, the need is so strong that it takes the form of spirit. A presence opens the door to my bedroom and floats through the room. I sense Mitchell's spirit climbing into Ben's body while we make love and the fantasy temporarily tames Linda's deepest desires. Ironically, the next day, I notice my lust for Mitchell detaches me from Ben's chaotic circle. My co-dependent nature fades away. So does my patience. I'm on edge. I snap easily.

Larry and I meet before the workday begins and sip coffee at a cozy cafe.

"I have these overwhelming feelings for Mitchell," I say. "I don't know what to do about it."

Larry hates hearing 'it.' He taps his right shoulder and then his left saying, "An angel sits on one side and the devil on another. You know what I mean? Don't go that way. You're only heading for trouble."

I try to block out Larry's elementary wisdom because *Linda* is bursting with grade school emotions. We quickly finish our coffees and race out the door to make it to the office on time.

On my way, I call Mitchell on my cell phone.

When he answers his deep voice vibrates my core.

"Mitchell," I say. "I need to tell you something."

He's expecting business talk but instead *Linda* blurts out, "I have a crush on you and I don't know what to do. I don't know what's happening to me," I explain. "I've always been crazy about my husband, but now I have feelings for you." I'm unprepared to hear Mitchell roar as if he has conquered a mate.

"I'm flattered," he says.

At this point, I'm not sure if I should be embarrassed or flattered that he's flattered. I need to find my composure.

"We have so much in common," he says. "I know what you mean."

He keeps talking but I can't comprehend his words. I'm temporarily in shock from my emotions spilling all over him. *Linda* needs to simmer. I hang up with an enormous sense of relief. There, I can function again.

Another burst of inspiration hits me but in a most tragic way just before Christmas. There is a death. My brother in-law's niece dies in a car accident. She is only seventeen. Nicky had been home on break from a performing arts school in New York. She was a most talented young lady who had sung and danced her way through life. Her friends truly loved her and it shows at her funeral. I sit in total amazement as I hear a recording of her angelic voice bursting through side speakers during the eulogy that day. I have never been so touched. It hits me very powerfully – I have to do something special with my life. I need to do something meaningful.

I'm bursting to share.
Something deep within is trying to surface.

Level III

*The third form of healing is a combination of
emotional and inner healing that integrates the
fragmented personality into one.
As they fold into one another,
the experience can be as frightening as dying.*

Chapter 9

Open to Receive

I'm stirring Grandma Marietta's red sauce recipe and with the kids calmly settled watching the purple dino-saur, when the phone suddenly rings.

"Hello?"

"Hi, it's Mitchell Gray."

I get comfortable and curl up on the couch to chat while Mitchell starts to talk.

"You know, you did such a great job. I managed to get you a little extra money in your bonus," he says. "I'm planning another trip very soon. How would you like to get together for drinks to celebrate your bonus?"

Linda uses the line she's rehearsed for weeks – "I'd love to," she says.

"Great," he says. "I'll be in town the week of the 29th. I'll call you ahead to schedule a day and time."

As days pass, I wrestle with guilty thoughts of actually meeting him. Is this what it feels like stepping into an affair? I know my intentions are wrong. They are wrong, just plain wrong. Why am I like this? I'm married – married for life, so I thought, but now the love is gone between Ben and me. His seductive energy no longer captivates me.

It was almost immediately when Mitchell's heartstring

securely held Linda from falling back into Ben's abusive cycle.
Do I tell my therapist or not? If I tell her, she will stop me.
Lord knows, Linda doesn't want to be stopped, yet I know I
need to be! I can't take it anymore.

It's a cold winter's day and I'm finding it humiliating to confess my intimate thoughts and feelings about Mitchell to my therapist.

A full-figured woman in her early forties, my therapist, Diane, uses her direct and deliberate approach to jolt me to my senses rather quickly.

"Before meeting him you must have an agenda," she says. "Make sure you make it very clear that you're not going to get involved. Otherwise, don't meet him. Make it very clear you are ending this."

"Ending what?" I ask. "Doesn't it take a sexual act to consummate an affair? I'm still safe, right? – I'm safe because nothing physical has happened, yet."

Diane's right. I have to end this before it starts. I have a
business reputation to protect. And the sad truth is that I'm
married to an alcoholic in a marriage that isn't going to last.
I need my livelihood to fall back on to care for my children. I
can't get involved with him. I have too much at stake and it's
not worth risking my career.

At the end of the therapy session, after Diane and I finish talking about my problems, she says, "Off the record...I have a business question for you. Because of managed care and cutbacks in the field of mental health I'm thinking about producing self-help tapes on relationships and raising teenagers. How do you suggest I market the tapes?"

I think about it for a second or two. "Well, I guess the

best way to market your tapes is in a self-help magazine,"
I say. "Wow, come to think of it...that's a great idea for a
magazine."

The sky is crystal blue and the air is crispy cold. The
thrill of the idea tickles my brain, as I speed down the
Eisenhower. There isn't a magazine designed to help
people cope with their problems. There's *Psychology
Today*, but it's too clinical. The other women's magazines
touch on self-help, but most are superficial, materialistic,
self-centered or old lady-ish. Not one is edited for someone like me.

That evening, Ben and I are cleaning up dishes
after dinner.

"What do you think about an idea for a self-help magazine?" I ask. "You know, a magazine that helps people get
through their problems."

"You mean, kind of like a 12–Step magazine?" asks Ben.

"Yes, like 12-Step," I answer.

Ben surprises me by saying, "I think that's a great idea. I
think that would really work."

I'm delighted yet shocked to see Ben supportive – let
alone, helping out with the dishes. I had expected the
opposite, and had prepared a kneejerk reaction to block
his critical energy.

"I'm going to call my friend David, at *Style Today*, and
run this idea by him," I say giving the sink a final rinse.
"He's worked on launch magazines before."

After I drop Lizzie at daycare and Michelle dozes off in
her car seat, I pick up my cell phone and start to dial 212.

"David Schwartz speaking."

"Hey David...it's Riley. You won't believe this...I have

an idea for a magazine." "Great...what is it?"

"It's a self-help magazine."

"Oh...like *Psychology Today*?"

"Well, kind of... but different because it's alive," *Linda* says with excitement. "It's about people telling their stories and how they work through problems and heal."

"Sounds great," he says. "Put your idea on paper. I'll read it and let you know if I can help spin it in a direction."

Ben buys our first personal computer – it's a Mac – and we place it on top of an old dining room table, shoved into the only available, cobweb-infested corner of our basement – where the floor is still cement. We conveniently plug it into a pre-existing three-prong outlet.

I work late at night when my kids are sleeping. As I begin to write, it comes easily – I'm writing from my heart, and not my head. This is embarrassing to admit, but it's as if I'm writing my thoughts to Mitchell, instead of David.

Mesmerized in the flow, I feel something greater is working through me. Linda reaches far up into the heavens as the inspiration flows. The sentences are popping rapidly, from my heart, up to my brain and my fingers can barely keep up.

I write about self-help books on bestseller lists, the increase in individual therapy sessions for the sake of personal growth, and several other market trends. I know the magazine is tapping into a movement led by women. It tickles me inside. I giggle out loud. I finish my last sentence saying, "Magazine X will be the premier personal growth magazine in the country."

During the four days it takes me to write the ideas, Ben

is mad – or, more likely scared, as he sees an unfamiliar spirit blazing through my eyes, teetering between inspiration and insanity. For me, it's like finding my wings to fly – my ticket to freedom! Putting my focus in a positive direction to help others is better than having an affair. The energy is *powerful*.

"You snuck out of bed and went down there and worked on it again," Ben says to me the next morning. "Didn't you?"

"I did," I admit. "Why should that bother you?" I ask.

"Because….you're acting crazy. I've never seen you like this."

"But you have your projects," I say in defense. "You've been tearing down walls and staying up until all hours."

The inspiration continues and floats into my dreams. During my twilight state, I capture treasures of fully composed rhythmic sentences – ones that I'd never create on my own – and then jot them down. The third night, while Ben and I lay in bed, he senses I'm a bit antsy for him to fall asleep.

"I know you're going to get this magazine published because this is a really good idea," he says. "You're going to sell this to somebody and then you're going to leave me."

"No, I'm not," I say.

But deep inside, I know he's right about the magazine and probably right about my leaving. The love in my heart for him is like a dried up old sponge – every droplet has been completely wrung out. The only lifeline that replenishes me is a magazine idea and a tiny string connecting me to a man I barely know.

To me, the hardest part about writing is spelling and punctuation. As a child, I was a natural at story writing and had a knack for remembering vivid colorful dreams.

How frustrating. I need to get this out while the conversation is still fresh. Spellcheck isn't working and I don't trust myself to proofread the work.

"Can you look at these pages before leaving?" I ask Ben as I follow him down the stairs early one morning. "I just need another set of eyes to correct the spelling because I really want to get this out today," I explain.

"No, I don't have time," Ben coldly replies.

"If you were really my friend you would want to help me; so I guess, you're really not my friend, are you?" *Linda* huffs back.

"I already read it," he says looking up at me from the landing. "It's fine...I've been correcting your mistakes all along the way," he adds condescendingly.

"I can't believe you did that!" *Linda* blurts with more hurt and anger bubbling over inside. "How dare you? Just forget it. I'll find someone else."

Level IV

*The fourth stage of healing is a final cleansing of
the heart/soul. It is a review of one's life that leads to
understanding and compassion of self as well as others.
This level achieves complete open-heartedness
in personal relationships and the world.*

Chapter 10

Somewhere, Out There

There's no better way to heal pain than by putting your focus on something greater than yourself. My purpose was to share the knowledge gained as I clawed my way out of a hole in search of emotional well-being. I learned the importance of breaking unhealthy cycles and knew from my own personal experience that stories shared were healing forces of the heart. It was doubly clear that, as we healed ourselves, we healed our children, who are the appendages of ourselves.

It was my heart's desire to help millions of women in search of emotional well-being by creating a magazine to inspire strength and courage; bring comfort and wisdom; and teach personal responsibility and "self-care" to nourish our lives.

"Hey, Riley...I heard you have an idea for a magazine," Mitchell says when he phones to confirm our date.

"How did you find out?" I ask in a paranoid tone. "I mean...who told you?"

"I bumped into your friend David at the Magazine Publisher's Association meeting last week down in Boca," Mitchell replies. "So, tell me...what's it about?"

"I can't say. It's very personal," *Linda* responds in a shy and embarrassed manner.

I'm not as ready to share my most intimate thoughts

with Mitchell as I was during my ecstatic nights
of creating.

"Then send it to me," he urges.

"No, no I can't," I say. I'm protective. "You can read it
when you come to town. Do you know, Jason, the mar-
keting director, at Gold Publishing, Inc.?"

"Sure...I've met him once or twice."

"He told me Gold is shopping for magazine ideas and
he thinks mine is very interesting."

"Wow...that's great."

Maybe Mitchell's not going to show? But I know he
checked in. I dropped off my magazine idea to him this
morning at the front desk.

I call up from the concierge's desk.

"Mitchell Grey, here," he says.

Thank God he's answered.

"Mitchell, I'm here," I say.

"Would you like to come up or would you like me to
come down to meet you?" he asks calmly.

*In the back of my mind, I hear Diane's voice warning me
not to go to his room. I hear her wisdom telling me, "Be careful, and remember, if anyone sees you, it can be held against
you."*

"How about you meet me down here," I say.

I wait, perched on the edge of the green velvet couch in
the lobby, while pretending to read a newspaper. Within
minutes, I can feel Mitchell walking towards me. I look
up. He's ten feet away, wearing a double-breasted dark
suit. I can tell his hair has been freshly cut and styled. It's
combed off to the side, not that messy boyish look.
We give each other soft cheek kisses and then stroll into

the lounge.

"I read your magazine idea and I think it's great," he says while handing back my document. "All the facts on mental health and personal growth were just fascinating...fascinating."

Right away Mitchell lights up a cigarette and says to the waitress, "I'll have a bourbon-on-the-rocks with a twist of lime."

Hmm...liquor...he drinks liquor. It makes me nervous; to be attracted to someone who likes to drink.

"Yes, and I'd like a Chardonnay," I say.

"So, do you have a name for the magazine?" Mitchell asks with a smile.

"Well...I can't think of a name so it's just called Magazine X for now."

"How about using a celebrity to host a column?" Mitchell suggests. "Like a radio talk show therapist."

"Wow...what a great idea," says *Linda*. "Who do you suggest?"

My hand shakes as I raise my glass, while my other hand comes up to steady the glass, hoping it goes unnoticed. I can't keep the conversation focused on business anymore. I need to tell Mitchell how sorry I am for confusing him.

"Listen, Mitchell," I say. "I really like you a lot and I know this isn't right – you know, I'm married and you're married – but sometimes, when people hurt inside they reach out." I've never shared the truth about my marriage with anyone outside the walls of a support group, my family, and a few close friends. "My career is very important to me," I tell him. "I need it to fall back on because my husband is an alcoholic." *Linda* reflects on the plot of *Beauty and the Beast* and intensely summarizes by saying, "...it's like living with a beast." I'm not sure if he fully understands, but it feels good to let Mitchell in and to spill my sorrow.

Mitchell pauses to take it all in. By the look on his face, he's searching to respond – somehow. "If I wasn't married, you would be someone I'd want to date," he says awkwardly.

"Me, too," I say giving him a warm smile.

We finish our drinks and walk to the lobby.

"I'll be back in town in two weeks," he says. "Can I see you again?"

"Sorry I'm out of town that week," I say, flustered with a false smile upon my face.

It's not easy refusing my only connection to love.

Level V

Finally, with open heart/soul, the integrated
self filters all mind activity down and
through the heart/soul and life becomes divine
as the authentic self is formed for service in the world.

Chapter 11

Bathroom Voices

Every crucial turning point in my life seems to revolve around our 1927 post-vintage mahogany table in our dining room. There I sit. It must be the look on my face Ben notices when he returns home from his trip out west. He walks in the door, puts down his bags, and catches disgust reflecting in my eyes. He pensively stares back.

"Are you having an affair?" he asks.

"No, I'm not," I say.

By this time, I'm conscious how truth moves me forward. I've been working hard at reaching deep in my heart. That's where I can feel it. I know my truth and my connection to God resides somewhere in the center of my chest and about eight inches down. Being honest within keeps my path straight and healthy inside. When I go against myself, I cause a battle inside, creating dis-ease.

"I have feelings for someone but I'm not having an affair. I would never do that," I admit.

He's goes crazy, crazy for days, until, finally, one morning he overhears me talking in my sleep. I'm dreaming about my cousin, Mick, who's a dentist, and we're mixing chemicals in a vial. Ben wakes me. It's 6 a.m.

"I know you're dreaming about him. I can hear you

calling someone's name." Ben demands, "Who is it?"
It's kind of eerie and it freaks me out that he invades my
dream world, especially since my cousin's name sounds
like Mitch. He rattles off names of a few close friends. "Is
it Tom, Ed, Leslie...?" he quizzes.

"No, no are you kidding. Are you crazy? A woman?"
I exclaim as I try holding back my laughter. It's getting
ridiculous, so ridiculous that I'm compelled to tell him
who it is – just to stop the nonsense. Besides, I'm not
having an affair. I ended it before it started.

I swallow a deep breath and ready myself like a cliff
diver about to jump into the ocean. What do I have to
lose other than the private fantasy of being with Mitchell in my mind? "It's Mitchell Gray," I confess. "He's not
from around here. It's harmless." In my righteous defense
I continue, "I'm entitled to have feelings. It's something
I can't control. But what I do have control over are my
actions and what I do with my feelings."

Relief settles in our bedroom for a brief moment.

Ben leaves to shower downstairs, and I'm still lying
in bed, barely able to pick my head up off the pillow. I
struggle to stand and slowly shuffle down the hall toward
the bathroom, and that's when it hits me – the feeling of
humility engulfs my entire body.

The kids are still sleeping. I take another laborious step
to enter into the shower and a second wave of humility
rolls through me. I start to shower. I can feel the pressure
between my eyes as tears run down my cheeks, mixing
with the water. As I lather more soap and rotate my body
to cleanse it, there's a moment when my mind takes a
short time-out. And in that *emptiness*, a voice enters the

left lower lobe of my brain.

"You will have a wonderful life," she says.

I ignore the voice, assuming it's a thought from within. When I hear it again, I ignore it.

"You will have a wonderful life," she says again.

This time, I hear it clearly. It sounds like the voice of a mother – soft and comforting. She tells me two more times. "You will have a wonderful life."

I count – one, two, three, four, five – and realize this is *real*.

The humility creates another opening and special grace is given like I've never known before. Her voice, so soothing and motherly, sounds like it could be that of *Mary*. She gives me peace and a sense of hope that my life is blessed on this day and several days to come. It isn't a guarantee of instant happiness – in fact, after receiving the message, the challenges become even harder. Yet, my faith grows stronger with her words permanently set in my mind to use as a guidepost marking my path.

Life is getting down to the nitty-gritty and my focus isn't on Ben anymore. It's about the baggage *Linda* brings up from her darkness. I hunker down and hold on tight, as my Catholic foundation kicks in to pull me through. For several years, I used to pray to God to make my husband sober and to watch over my children, but now I'm praying for myself. Every morning and night, with the covers up over my head, *Linda* recites *The Lord's Prayer*, my heart intimately connecting to His spirit. I pray to take away the forbidden love that holds my heart and to give me direction and purpose in my life.

A deeper meaning comes from within, as I reflect on

the words, "You will have a wonderful life." It becomes
the gentle nudge I need to continue my work and to try
to put aside my feelings for Mitchell. I take the next step
to keep the momentum going by arranging a meeting
with Jason at Gold.

"On vacation, Ben picks an elegant setting for lunch
to tell me he loves me and then boom, he tells me he
bought a new boat – a $120,000 new boat," I tell Sylvia,
our new marriage therapist. "I'm shocked he has the
nerve to make a decision that large, without me, and a
decision we can't afford."

"Ben...how did you think Riley would react?" asks
Sylvia.

"I thought it would be great for the family...we needed
a bigger boat. I thought she'd be excited since we were
already shopping for a bigger boat," Ben says.

"We were looking for a used boat. Not a new one.
There's a big difference," I exclaim. Besides, my dream is
to buy a new house, not a new boat." I explain further,
"We live on a corner next to the park at Lincoln and
Ridge. I'm always afraid of the kids running in the street
or getting kidnapped from our yard."

"Ben, do you see why Riley is upset?"

"Oh, all she cares about is that damn magazine...she's
obsessed with the magazine," Ben huffs. "And to top
it off, she likes this guy Mitchell Gray who smokes
and drinks."

I cringe listening to him. My attention is redirected.
I've never noticed this before, but I can see peace emanat-
ing from the therapist's eyes. Intrigued by her sense of
calm, I secretly wonder if I can attain that look someday.

The therapist, intrigued as well with the conversation about the magazine, recommends we read *The Celestine Prophecy.*

The next few sessions result in a circle of endless arguments. Ben seems to be working hard at making it not work – and a waste of money. Finally, he and I agree on one thing, the therapy isn't working.

Jason is a thin-faced man in his early forties, hiding behind wire-framed glasses and with streaks of gray flowing from his crown.

"Come on in...please have a seat...can I get you some coffee?" he graciously gestures.

"Oh, no thank you. I think I have way too much energy as it is," I say, holding a big smile.

I can feel the excitement come up inside as I bring out my presentation folder and unfold it over the oval table. I've done a million presentations for other publishers' magazines, but this time is different, because it's my baby and everything comes naturally.

Jason follows the presentation intently. When I get to the psycho-jargon part about the individuation-stage-of-adulthood his face reveals how it has something to do with him. My conviction is strong throughout. At the end of the presentation *Linda* is pounding on his desk. "This magazine *will* get published and I know it!" she says. I've never pounded on someone's table before and the words come out with such determination. Jason is just as intense as I am.

"I'm sure it will!" He pauses, briefly holding his index finger pressed against his lips. "I have to think about whether I can take on another project. Give me three

weeks to make a decision before you go anywhere else."
He shifts the tone of the conversation to business.

"So, what's your role?" he asks.

"What do you mean?" I naively ask.

"Do you want to be the publisher?" he asks.

"Publisher? I never thought about it. I just want to get
the magazine published," I say.

Our Father

Our Father, who art in heaven;
Hallowed be Thy name;
Thy kingdom come;
Thy will be done on earth as it is in heaven.
Give us this day our daily bread;
And forgive us our trespasses
As we forgive those who trespass against us,
And lead us not into temptation;
But deliver us from evil.
Amen.

– Jesus Christ

Chapter 12

The Storm

At the end of three weeks, Jason's answer is, simply, "My plate is too full." It's a nice safe way to let me down gently. "I like the idea, but there are other magazines I'm committed to that are further along in the development stage," he explains.

"I understand," I say. But really, it's hard to take. I'm disappointed.

"You need a business plan and an editor," he says.

We kick off the summer with a half-birthday party for our two girls whose birthdays are in December. At the end of the day, Ben prepares a delightful grilled salmon with angel hair pasta dinner. Then he surprises my mother and me with our own bottle of Chardonnay. He pours us both a glass. It's a nice gesture, but I couldn't care less about drinking. And, besides, it's a little strange, especially since Ben's been sober a year. Right away, it makes me feel on edge.

"Oh, so you bought wine?" I nervously ask, as he pours.

"Yes and I'm drinking non-alcoholic wine for myself," Ben explains. "I want this to be a nice occasion for all of us."

Earlier, I had detected a little-too-happy-jump in his step and now my antenna is on full alert. Whenever Ben is too up or too nice, it means he's drinking or on drugs.

Today also is the beginning of our weekend voyage on the new boat – we planned for the kids to stay home with my mom. As each half hour passes, between dinner and packing the car, I'm convinced he's drinking the non-alcoholic wine to camouflage drinking the 'real stuff.' I hold back confronting him because I don't want to be accusatory. If this is a relapse, it's very serious for Ben, the children, and me. I don't want him around the children if it's really happening. I'm capable of handling the situation better alone.

We get in the car and he wants to drive to the marina.

"Nope. I'm driving," I say.

We switch places. Another clue. Usually he'd be obstinate and say, "No. I'm driving."

Again, this is very serious. I feel I need to be absolutely sure before accusing him. I pull out onto the main road. A flashback comes to me – when Ben's buzzed, he likes to put in a CD and sing.

As he sings, he gives me one of those "Ooh, we're on our way," looks and I think, "Oh, oh, oh. Not really."

Then, just before turning right, onto the next main road, I look at him. "I know. I know you've been drinking," I say.

He denies it.

I watch his body language. I can tell by the way he tips his head to the side and the awkward shuffling of his arms that I'm right. The rest of the forty-five minutes on the road is silent.

The rule of thumb is – if you think it is; it is when living with an addict.

A few minutes before arriving at the yacht club, we ar-
gue about my obsession with the magazine and falling for
someone else. By this time, it's dark as I pull in front of
the dock to unload everything from the car to the boat.

"That f---ing Mitchell B. Gray," Ben bawls before getting
out of the car.

I freeze. How does he know his middle initial? He must
have looked at the masthead of the magazine. I wonder.
Did he call Mitchell and tell him to back off? Is that
why Mitchell never called back? Ben is so conniving and
sneaky about everything, I wouldn't put it past him. He
could have left a message on his voice mail. I'm in shock.

We unload everything from the car to the boat.

"We're not going anywhere until the morning, until
you're sober," I say in disgust.

Ben goes stiff and passes out in the V berth.

After he falls asleep, I can't sleep. I lie in a separate
bunk on the opposite end of the boat and try to fall
asleep. I can't. I'm so upset. I try holding back my tears
but I really need to cry and I need to do it in solitude. I
quietly leave the cabin, drive down the street to the party
store and buy cigarettes. Then I drive to another marina
parking lot, where I sit behind the wheel, just bawling
my eyes out. I just cry.

Once I calm down and think things over, I decide to
stay and try to enjoy the weekend. What more can happen? It can't get any worse. I return to the boat and pray
myself asleep.

Even though we hear the weather forecast announcing
storm warnings, we still take off in the morning – and,

from that moment on, I slip further into depression.
I close my eyes and lie on the back of the boat thinking about Mitchell. It makes me feels good to drift into
another world and completely block out Ben. I'm sure he
feels the disconnection.

We travel south towards Indiana and it starts raining.
We first make our way by hugging the coastline before
motoring across to our destination, Saugatuck, a quaint
little town on the Michigan side. The rain disappears and
the heavy grey clouds lighten to white, so we decide to go
for it. We follow the map, pinpoint the landmarks, and
turn the vessel straight into the vast waters, heading for
the Michigan shoreline. The wind kicks up, and almost
instantly, we are in the middle of ten-foot swells.

It reminds me of my childhood, and the many times
my father used to navigate our family through the treach-
erous storms of Lake St. Clair. We would always head
toward Canada and land safely on her shores, for shelter.

I can feel *Linda* steering inside, as Ben and I take turns
driving the boat. I'm getting really sick.

"Look," *Linda* says to Ben. "I have to drive. It'll help me
get over feeling so sick. I mean, if I can just stay focused
on the waves, I'll do better."

Ben lets *Linda* drive.

"How are you feeling," Ben yells, holding tight in the
passenger seat.

"Much better," I say smiling with the wind separating
my eyelashes. I like being behind the wheel. I like being in charge. It comforts me. "How about you...are you
okay?" I yell back.

"Yes, I'm great. Now just keep the boat pointed to the
right and ride the waves on an angle," Ben explains.

"There's land...I see land," *Linda* says excitedly. "How about you take over? I don't know how to bring the boat in,"

From two steps back, I can see more clearly. God answers my prayer from the night before by showing me how to break through the cycle of alcohol abuse.

The answer is – when *Linda* takes control and focuses, I'm no longer sick anymore. I do have control over something...it's me.

Chapter 13

Faltering Footsteps

Everything spins out of control as I spend an entire summer watching Ben's pitiful cycle – three weeks on, three weeks off. I struggle to find solid footing. The kids are feeling the dysfunction too. I can't help but notice weary signs surface upon their little faces as they cringe each time Ben and I fight. Even when we're not arguing, the tension between us is thick. When Ben's not using, I'm paranoid he will; and when he is, I'm thinking of ways to protect us from him.

One afternoon, while barbecuing, Ben excuses himself to step out and buy beer for our friend Jim and something non-alcoholic for himself. About an hour later, he's back from the store *drunk*.

Oh no!! I'm back in the cycle. I feel like a victim again, and it doesn't make a bit of difference what I do or how I act. He still drinks. It has nothing to do with me. My heart sinks to my stomach and tears well up in my eyes.

"Stay strong," my mother says holding up both my shoulders.

"I don't know how," I cry and shake my head from side to side saying, "...not anymore."

The last thing I want is to break up my young family. I

think back on the message God tried to show me the day of the storm. It's Linda who drives the boat and focuses on the waves to keep from getting sick. I need her back. I need to get the focus back on me and my magazine. It's the only thing that frees my spirit, gives me life and removes me from Ben's chaotic circle without breaking up my family.

I can still hear Jason's words, "You need a business plan and an editor," so I take a step forward by contacting John, from Style Today. We worked together a few years ago and I'm hoping he remembers.

"John Greenlees," he answers.

"Hi John...this is Riley."

"Oh, yes." he says, "It's been a long time. How are you doing?"

"Just fine...listen, I have an idea for a magazine but I really need to find an editor..." and then I explain where I left off with Gold. "It's a magazine on personal growth," I continue on with great enthusiasm. "...a woman's magazine, unlike any other."

"Oh...that sounds great. I know someone just right for this," he says. "Let me talk to her first, and then I'll put you two together."

Next, I think about Mitchell. I'm sure he knows how to write a business plan but I can't run the risk of Ben finding out that I'm talking to him.

Honestly, to this day, I still have a hard time understanding what draws me to Mitchell. It's a complete mystery how I feel imaginary strings lacing through the opening in my wounded heart to Mitchell's, held together by Linda's love. The hard part about all of this is that the strings never fully connect. There's a constant dull aching pain, located at the surface of my chest, as if something is unable to break through. Perhaps

*it's displaced trauma – you know, when you go to a doctor
and you say, "The pain is here." But the doctor says, "No. It's
really here." I seriously question whether I'm going through a
midlife crisis, while going through a crisis. I'm so frustrated
with half-baked therapists who can't dish out straight answers. I'm so sick of being asked, "How does that make you
feel?" I need to take control of my life and find the answers to
my own questions – it's my responsibility.*

I decide to call John again.

"I'm sorry it took so long to get back to you," John
apologizes.

"Hey, did you ever get a hold of your editor friend?"

"I have a better idea," he says excitedly. "Are you talking to anyone else at this time?"

"No...not right now," I say wondering where he's going
with this.

"Good, because I want you to bring it to us," he says.
"Larry Olsen is the person you need to contact. He's in
charge of magazine development. He will be expecting
your call."

Linda's ecstatic and hangs up immediately to call Larry.

Right off the bat, Larry says, "I'd like you to sign a confidentiality agreement."

"Sorry...I can't do that," *Linda* quickly responds. "What
I have is unlike any women's magazine."

"You can't send it unless you sign one," Larry
continues.

"Then I'll come show it to you," says *Linda*.

*More than anything, I'm determined to get my magazine
published. I have to. It's my lifeline. It's my purpose. It's keeping me together, giving me balance, holding off my depression.
For now it's my best medicine.*

Once into the presentation, Larry forgets to have
me sign the confidentiality agreement. He loves
every minute.

"This is great," Larry says, as he practically twirls in his
seat. "Will you leave this with me?"

"No," *Linda* says with a smile. "I can't."

"Well, listen," he says. "I need to talk to management.
We need to make a decision. I'll let you know
right away."

A week later – "You're not talking to anyone else yet?"
Larry asks.

"No. Just you," I answer.

"I need another week," he says. "We're in the middle of
mergers. I'll call you back."

Someone announces in the managers meeting, "*Taste
of Chicago* is a great event to invite your publisher or ad
director to come to town to see." When I hear the words,
Linda immediately gets the feeling that Mitchell will
be there.

*The endless aching in my heart never subsided, for a love
lost and one never gained.* My emotions remain ensnared
between Ben and Mitchell.

This particular morning, I wake with a sick stomach.
I'm convinced that I'm going to see him today. I slip into
my sharpest navy blue suit and take extra care applying
makeup and fixing my hair.

On my way in, I listen to the words of a song, "I don't
want to wait for your love anymore." Underneath my
heartache, I wonder if I'm a fool waiting for Mitchell. I
can't help it, each time I think of Mitchell, I get a feeling
of love. I guess I do it out of habit – it's a guaranteed 'feel

good' in my 'feel bad' world.

I remember that I don't have the leave-behind materials for my meeting. Quickly, I park the car, dash to the office, and run down the hall to snatch the material off my desk.

In the conference room, across from my office, I hear a man's deep rumbling voice similar to Mitchell's. I feel completely undone with my heart falling somewhere in my stomach and my lungs gasping for air.

Linda curses, "Oh shit," as she stumbles through the door, falls in her chair and searches the desk top for the leave-behinds. I was right – Mitchell's here. I've got to get the hell out of here for the sake of my dignity.

After my meeting, Linda protests, "I can't go back to the office," so we hide out in a coffee shop like a wounded animal in the brush. It's my time to adjust. Bring myself back together. I need to face him. To find the answers to my questions – Why he holds this mysterious power over me? Why he shakes my core? And, is it love?

I catch Mitchell from afar getting out of a cab, a few cars in front of me. I give him a little time to acclimate.

Okay. I'll break the ice. I'll go up to him and say 'hello' because I don't think he sees me. My whole body begins to shake. "Go ahead, it can't be that noticeable," I prod Linda.

I walk up to him, hold out my hand to shake his and say, "Hi. How are you?" I can feel my mouth dry and my top lip is sticking to my front teeth. I must look like an idiot...a complete idiot.

"Oh...Riley...it's great to see you," he says with a handshake that's as exciting as a piece of cold shrimp.

How embarrassing. He seems disinterested. I watch him peer over the top of my head, as if he's looking for someone more important than me. Last time, I recall, we melted into each other's eyes before parting. I can't take it anymore. So in the middle of my third sentence, with my lip still sticking to my teeth, Linda takes a twirl and walks away. I feel like a complete nincompoop to have misread these feelings for love. I'm better off to clean my hands of everything. Oddly enough, maybe his rejection is the reality check I need to help one get rid of this curse; the curse that holds me back from facing the real problem...me.

Next, I enter *Taste of Chicago's* elaborate food demonstration events. Mitchell is seated in the first row, with an empty seat next to him. He spots me walking in. "Riley... Come here," he says motioning to me. "Come...sit here."

Linda is elated, forgetting his cold-handed reception minutes ago. She scoots around the people standing in the way and slides in next to him.

"Good to see you again," he says softly while staring with his deer brown eyes.

"Nice to see you too," I reply. This time, I'm okay. My teeth aren't sticking anymore.

"How's it going with your magazine?" he asks.

"I've been talking to American Publishers. They're supposed to let me know sometime later this week."

"That's wonderful," he says. "And what about Jason at Gold...Are you still talking to him?"

"No...Jason couldn't take it on," I say disappointedly. "But I'm writing a more extensive business plan. Have you ever written one before?"

"Sure...give me a call. I'd be happy to help you."

What a guilt-free, glorious afternoon playing *Taste of Chicago* with Mitchell Gray. Yet, I still can't figure him out.

At one point, he looks at me and says, "I really admire you." Then he asks, "Why didn't you call me when you were in New York?"

"I did, but you never returned my call," I say with the hurt still stuck in my throat.

He looks miffed.

At the end of the day we share a cab ride back to the office. Feeling curious, I take a brief moment to gaze at Mitchell. With only a few short minutes left, I scan him from top to bottom. I take in everything, from his handsomely shaped head, to his thick brown shiny hair, his natural scent and polished mannerisms. My effort is completely in vain. What is it? The answer comes quickly: It's not one thing – it's *everything*.

Before we get out of the cab, he takes my hand and stares into my eyes. "It's always a pleasure being with you," he says.

"Yes it is," says my enchanted *Linda*.

Chapter 14

The Furnace Repair

"Upper management doesn't understand your magazine concept. I'm sorry, we can't take on the project," Larry lets me know, sounding disappointed as if it's his failure. I can't help but think, whoever upper management is, they're fools for not recognizing the importance and viability of *Advice*.

That same week, Ben is drunk handing out candy on Halloween. Lucky for me, this time I can't feel it puncture my heart because it's shielded by Mitchell's energy still lingering from the week before. I'm determined to keep going with *Advice*. Gold and American Publisher aren't the only publishers out there.

"Hello...Mitchell Gray speaking."

"It's Riley."

"Oh...nice to hear from you...you know, I really enjoyed being with you," he says with words from the heart. I close my eyes to take in his sweetness.

"When are you coming back?" I ask.

"I don't know," he answers and then there's awkward silence.

Before hanging up I ask, "Mitchell, would you mind if I sent you my magazine presentation deck? I'd love to hear your thoughts."

The following week, I call him back.

"It's a real page turner," says Mitchell.

"Oh...thank you," I say, "Do you think I need to do anything else?"

"No, it's fine. Don't worry. Something will come of it. If it's not this, it will be something else...just keep going."

"So, are you coming to the Christmas party?"

"No, I can't," he says. Suddenly, I feel a wall go up.

"You came to the Christmas party last year," I remind him. "All your best clients will be there."

"I'll try...but I doubt it. It's too close to my Dallas trip."

After I hang up, the pain pushes up deep from the center of my chest. And after a couple of days, Mitchell's disconnection slowly settles in, so much so that I slither down deeper into the crevice of my heart – the one he first opened. I feel empty, between loves lost and loves never gained. Within days, I *collapse*.

My health plummets with a bout of the flu, yet my will remains strong. I tell myself that I'm going to get better. I'll be at the Christmas party and he'll show up. But there is a force much stronger than me, keeping me down. It's almost as if I'm deliberately being held down until the day the party passes. Then, I recover – but only temporarily. It's enough to get me back on my feet, to finish buying toys for the kids. After the holidays, I collapse again. This time I'm diagnosed with walking pneumonia and my doctor puts me on a regimen of heavy antibiotics and steroids.

Ben actually cares for me, as I cough and struggle repeatedly to catch my breath. Then loneliness sets in that turns from depression to despair. I feel lonely inside but my family surrounds me. How can I be lonely? When my father died, I was in depression for a whole year before climbing out. I never went into therapy. I know the signs of falling in – of feeling empty, withdrawn, and tired all the time. Once you get in, it feels almost impossible to get out. I need professional help. I don't want to see any more psychotherapists. I need medical help. I have to get myself out, before I go in too deep – and the magazine isn't pulling me out anymore. Neither is Mitchell.

The challenge is to move through life – not to build-up, stack, block, avoid, or go around the pain. Emotional healing is about releasing the junk stuffed down inside. For me, it took a long time to learn: the deeper the pain, the better progress I was making. At least I feel it. After emotions release, it's God's grace that heals the tenderness within and new levels of awareness form.

The last place I want to be is back in therapy. But I'm sick of being depressed and having to deal with my problems on my own. I go for the quick fix.

"I want to go on Prozac," I say, hoping to hear the doctor say yes.

"Your depression is situational," he says instead. "You won't need medication to help you through."

To my surprise, every story of woe I tell frees my blockage. The doctor helps me discover the normal and not-so-normal behavior of Ben, my father and me.

"I want to fly away and run to Mitchell," I say.

"Why do you want to go into the fire?" the doctor asks. "You need to take care of the problem in front of you – the answers are inside."

But I can't face the inferno inside of me anymore. I know where it leads. I feel the pull of the doctor, redirecting me away from my passions and steering me towards divorce. This isn't the direction my soul dares to travel. I can't even say the word "divorce" – I just call it the "big D word." It definitely isn't in my vocabulary. And, besides, I'm Catholic. I promised my bridegroom ten years ago, "Once I marry, I marry for life." Even if it was an option, I'm not ready to take the leap – I have three little children to support.

No doubt, my thoughts of Mitchell are causing heartache-on-top-of-heartache. Running into the arms of someone unavailable is like alcohol to the alcoholic. As I heal one layer, the pain lessens and then I'm able to move deeper into the next layer. Each time I release small measures of toxic emotion, I realize it has little to do with the pain of a love never gained. Actually, the release of anger and hurt lessen my 'neediness' and I eventually eliminate the forever hole in my heart. But, honestly, it takes several years to free myself – and using a magazine and this book are simply my healing tools.

The doctor never warns me about the anger's afterglow. On the drive home, I have time to process thoughts. Unfortunately, Ben's car is in the drive when I pull up. The minute I walk in the door, he's there. I take one look at him and hatred rises in me instantly. That's when I turn into vigilante *Linda*, popping her head up and out of my stomach, hissing at Ben like a serpent spewing venom.

"How could you abandon us like that? Why didn't you go to the emergency room with Michelle? You put our lives in danger."

For years I pushed the hurt far down inside – and now that it's coming out, it's so lethal, so toxic, that you can see the fire's flames as Linda opens her mouth.

Ben is stunned and doesn't say a word. A few hours later, once I've calmed down, he tells me, "I've decided to move out for awhile. I don't feel loved."

Silently, I'm relieved. I don't say a word.

After Ben moves out, *Linda* finds the next victim to attack: my mother.

"Don't you remember?" I scream. "Every Christmas, Dad walked out on us."

"Oh, forget about that," she says brushing it off.

"I can't," yells *Linda*.

I remember that, as a child, I could smell the stench of beer on my father's breath while I pulled his ear lobes and tried to lift his eyelids to wake him to open presents Christmas Day.

"Don't you remember? We begged him to get help and then he died," I sob.

Next, my brother calls to calm me.

"Remember?...He beat you with a belt for poor grades!" I yell into the phone. "I saw him do it."

My brother laughs and says, "Yeah, but you didn't know I had a book stuffed in my pants."

"You did?" I say.

"He didn't hurt me and I faked my crying."

"And all these years, I've been feeling sorry for you."

He laughs out loud again.

"You know what?" my brother says. "It's time to stop. Stop with your anger therapy. This doctor is taking you for a ride at $170 a crack."

"But I'm so mad," I scream. "Our dad was a bad guy and so is Ben."

"I've forgiven Dad. Everyday, I thank him for being tough on me. I was out of control. Come on, you've got to move on."

"Really...you've forgiven him?"

Linda lashes out, with one last retaliation, by purchasing a mink coat and an expensive pair of Italian loafers to even the score with Ben for buying the boat.

Huh, she thinks. Take that. There. Yeah, that's my cure for moving on.

Later that day, curled up in my favorite barrel chair in the living room, I read something Judy Collins wrote. She says, "The richness that I have in my life is made up of a double journey, one into the past and the one into the future; the destination of those two journeys is always the present."

Something deep inside clicks...my brother's right...I'm done with anger therapy. I have to put my sights on the future to recapture my balance. Instead, the remaining anger the doctor wants me to unload, I channel in a positive direction to move the magazine project forward. With regard to Mitchell, I need to go deeper within – to find the answer to the mysterious connection between us on my own.

Chapter 15

Balance Beams

Actually, while in anger therapy, I discovered something else. The clue to being emotionally off-balance is
being physically off balance. I couldn't hit a straight ball
during tennis lessons.

Now, from thirty feet away, I see a familiar person
crouching down in front of the Shoe Gallery window on
Michigan Avenue. I'm on my way to return that pair of
Italian loafers, pushing Michelle in her stroller.

I stop to stare at George until he notices.

"Well, well," George says as he turns his head up.
"Riles...I haven't seen you in years." We hug and then
he looks me up and down. "What have you been doing?
How come you're so skinny?"

"I was working on my magazine but then I got
real sick."

George pulls out his business card and hands it to me.
"Let's meet for breakfast," he says. "I'd love to see your
plans for the magazine."

George stands up from the table as I walk in. He's a
handsome man in his mid-fifties, wearing a snappy looking, navy pinstriped suit that complements his curly

reddish-brown hair.

"I know I have something," I say, going through the presentation deck.

"I see what you mean," George says, staring straight at me. "This magazine has a real purpose," he says while pointing at the tag line that reads: *The Magazine of Personal Growth*.

"Ben thinks I'm a crazy obsessed woman...maybe I need a real job."

"No. This is your real job!" he says, pounding on the table. "Working on the magazine is your full-time job."

"Okay, you're with me on this? Right, George? I don't want to go it alone anymore."

"Yes, I'm in," he says.

It's evident how much George reminds Linda of the father she always yearned to have. He's so willing to share his wisdom and teach her his street smarts. She imagines her father would have been like him, if the demons of alcoholism hadn't devoured his spirit.

Thereafter, every week, we meet at the diner on State and Lower Wacker Drive to measure my progress on the magazine. George doesn't claim a part; all he wants is to pull me up and move me forward.

From that point, I decide to connect with Mitchell again, keeping a higher purpose in mind. I say a little prayer and dial his number.

"Mitchell Gray," he answers in his deep rumbling voice.

"Hi, Mitchell," I say quickly. "It's Riley. Hey, I'm stuck. Can you help me with the business plan?"

"Get a piece of paper and pen," he says. Then he takes forty-five minutes to dictate an outline. We don't linger in conversation beyond business, although he lingers in

.

my thoughts.

For days I work on the plan and feel my confidence rise as I contact Jason again. I say another little prayer while I dial his number.

"Listen. I've never stopped working on this," I say. "I'm really moving along and I've got Dr. Sara Reynolds, a radio talk show therapist, on board."

He doesn't know who Dr. Reynolds is – so *Linda* gives him a little spiel about her popularity on the coast and about her radio show reaching heights of national exposure.

"You know, she's all about personal responsibility," *Linda* says. "I think Dr. Reynolds makes a great contributing editor for *Advice*. She even agreed to transcribe live dialogue from the show in the pages of the magazine."

Linda has his attention now.

"You know," he says, "you still need an editor."

"I don't need an editor," *Linda* says. "It will slow me down. I'm ready, now! I have a table of contents and an art director creating a cover."

"You need an editor!" Jason repeats. "I know a woman editor who would be interesting for you to speak with."

Maybe he's right. It would free up my time to finish the business plan.

"Okay, I'll talk to her."

Priscilla and I first meet over the phone. With over fifteen years of magazine editing experience, Priscilla has recently ended a stint as executive editor of a service magazine. We talk at length about the mission of *Advice* and she is eager to take on the project. She agrees to work for free because Jason put us together – giving us a guaranteed captive audience at Gold Publishing, Inc.

Surprisingly, over time our conversations grow more and more frustrating as I explain the same thing numerous different ways. Finally, I realize Priscilla doesn't connect with the concept.

"What's the hold up?" Linda exclaims to Riley. "I've given her everything she needs! All she has to do is give it a spin, an editor's flair – it's all very simple!"

"Why don't I come and meet you," I suggest. "We can spend time together to go over the magazine concept." She agrees, so we plan the dates.

Perhaps it's also a very good time to dissolve my fantasies about Mitchell – the dream of flying away and running into his arms. Now that I'm feeling stronger, it's imperative I resolve the painful turmoil going on in my heart. I've sorted out enough to know my heartache keeps me from making sound judgments about my relationship with Ben. I find myself thinking about Mitchell to feel good, but the opposite happens after the thought. I feel pain come up. Maybe that's why my heart aches. It's the pain that keeps pushing up and wanting to come out about Ben and my father. Maybe when I think of Mitchell, my heart opens a wee bit, allowing the pain to surface about Ben and my father. But then I push it back down. Oh, it's all very confusing.

The bottom line is: "All blocks need to go away!" I yell out to Linda. I need to clear my mind and heart for important decisions that lie ahead. Perhaps divorce is the direction but all illusions of love must be eliminated.

"I feel like I'm with the wrong person," I say to George, during our weekly breakfast meeting.

"Maybe you need to share a bed with Mitchell in a

hotel room to resolve your problem," George suggests. "Sometimes, the reality of the situation will straighten you out more quickly."

"Are you serious? I can't imagine," I reply.

My reality is that I don't need more junk-on-top-of-junk-on-top-of-junk to confuse me even more. It's Eleanor Roosevelt who once said: "You gain strength, courage and confidence by every experience in which you really stop to look fear in the face."

How terrible to allow fear to hold me back. If I'm in love with somebody I hardly know, it's important to find out why. Otherwise, I'm always going to be stuck.

The rest of Eleanor's quote runs through my head: "You are able to say to yourself, 'I've lived through this horror. I can take the next thing that comes along.' You must do the thing you think you cannot do."

That's really what it comes down to. I've been stuck – in the fantasy of love for over a year. That's stupid. That's dumb. I have to take the next step. I have to take a chance and find out why. Maybe, Mitchell's an alcoholic like Ben and my father. Or, maybe, like me, he's the child of an alcoholic. Perhaps we hold the same energy stuffed down inside – similar to Linda's inferno – causing a mysterious connection, similar to pain breeding pain. Whatever it is, I need to move beyond the fascination in order to move forward.

With the help of a little prayer, I phone Mitchell.

"Mitchell, I'm coming to New York in a couple weeks," I say. "Can we meet to go over the business plan?"

"Oh, I can't that day. I have another obligation," he says.

My heart sinks. I'm determined. I can't afford *no*. No

doesn't give me closure; no doesn't free me; no is totally unacceptable.

I use every surface tactic to convince him to meet. *Linda* even uses George's suggestion, alluding to a weekend rendezvous. He's not budging. Finally, I take *the divine dive*, down to the base of my core for the fearless search for truth. A *transformation* occurs. It travels back up with God reaching through me. "We have to meet! It's important," I insist. Then, I pause, holding the *silence* until he agrees to give in.

Chapter 16

Run Away, Linda

Once the plane lands, I immediately run to a pay phone to call Mitchell. "I'm sorry," I apologize. "My plane was late taking off."

"No problem. Where do you want to meet?" asks Mitchell.

"Well, I need to drop my luggage at my girlfriend's," I explain.

"Great," he says. "We can meet there and then walk to the restaurant."

In the cab, with a view of Manhattan's skyline in front of me, a rush of energy zips through my body with a powerful sexual charge – about ten times more intense than the usual surge of hormones for a woman my age. The power is so strong that it scares me. Wow, this is dangerous. I can't meet him like this.

When the cab pulls up, he stands waiting in front of the building sucking down the last drag of his cigarette. I get out of the cab and walk toward him. His face looks very nervous and I see he's gained weight. As I walk closer, we simultaneously smile at each other. I feel immediately at ease. Then we lean for an exchange of friendly hugs. By this time, the evil energy has dissolved out of my body. He takes my bags into the lobby of my girlfriend's apartment. We leave them with the bellman and walk to the restaurant.

On the way, Mitchell is still very nervous, so I do most of the talking, about business, and about my frustrations with Priscilla. Since it's a late lunch, we're the only ones in the restaurant, except for an odd-looking woman in her fifties wearing glasses and a hat. She sits about three tables over from us, against the wall, reading a book.

Linda's suspicious. She thinks, "That woman is the spy Ben sent to follow me." For several weeks, Linda has a nagging feeling that my office is bugged. Ben monitors her every move.

Linda pulls out her business plan for Mitchell to review and he makes a few suggestions. After that, a strong feeling comes over her. "Mitchell, you need to be a publisher," she says. Surprised by her comment, Mitchell stays quiet.

As the master of a million questions, he shifts the conversation. We talk about my struggles. "You should stay off the antidepressants," he says. "They're just not good for you."

"What about you? What do you struggle with?" I ask in search of the mysterious connection.

"It's my weight," he says embarrassed. He's a bit heavier than before, but that's not the answer I'm looking for. Mitchell is private. He won't let me in any further.

"Do you love Ben?" he asks.

Surprisingly, no one ever asked before.

"No, I don't and I don't plan on being married to him the rest of my life," I say with certainty, surprising myself.

I get serious and then lean in.

"You know, I really like you," I say softly. "I like you

a lot."

"I like you a lot, too," he quickly responds. We pause. We stare.

Drawn in by his deep gentle eyes, I want to hold his hand. Instead, I use my left hand to hold my right hand back from reaching out to touch his – partly because the quirky woman reading the book against the wall is a reminder to be cautious. There. I'm successful at holding back physically, but the power between us is much stronger than me. My spirit moves out of my body and into his spirit – with both energy fields twirling together, between us. The mystery reveals itself. What I feel is *real*. It's love. I rest in peace. The imaginary heartstrings finally connect and the empty crevice that once pained my heart fills with God's love, delivered by Mitchell. This *love* becomes my lifeline for survival, without which, I feel I'd slowly die.

Mitchell jumps several steps ahead of me. "I could... I could never leave my family," he says, looking into my eyes that silently must have begged the answer.

I have to let go.

Left only with the love, I gain strength and courage to escape the emotional rollercoaster ride of Ben's alcoholism and to finish my mission.

No lingering good-byes or colliding hearts this time.

His gift of love touches me forever.

The next morning, I take a cab to Priscilla's apartment about fifteen minutes away. She's a petite, delicate-looking woman, with a porcelain-like complexion, probably in her late forties. She lives in a five-story, quaint brownstone with her husband and two little boys – one about my son's age and the other a couple of years older. Her apartment is full of old oriental rugs, antique furniture, and crystal chandeliers. I can't help but be impressed. They must have a lot of money to live in a lavish place like this on the Upper East Side of New York.

She invites me to take a seat on an old tapestry couch, in the extended bay area of the living room. *Linda* is thrilled to sing her passion about the magazine to Priscilla, who is so willing to listen and follow her every word with genuine interest. The poor woman, she'll never be able to shut her up. Back home, no one lets *Linda* talk about the magazine anymore. My friends and family – they're sick of hearing about it; it's almost embarrassing to even mention it unless they ask first.

The next morning we take off to their country home and it's a beautiful ride all the way up, but I barely take time to enjoy the scenery – we're so busy brainstorming about the magazine. Priscilla writes hurriedly, taking fast notes to catch *Linda's* every word as she explains, "This is a transformation magazine. It's about people going through a metamorphosis." I feel weird using heavy-imagery words to describe the magazine, but they seem to fit – especially since I recently went through a metamorphosis myself.

Because of my own experience, I'm very sensitive to any sort of dysfunction in a home. There's a lot of tension in Priscilla's marriage and with her children. I note that she's very nice to me but not so nice to them. As soon as I retire to the bedroom and shut the door, she screams at the top of her lungs at her gracious husband and sweet little boys. *Linda* blocks the rest of Priscilla's screaming with her headphones tucked inside her ears, listening to sappy songs.

Over time, I share my secret with Priscilla about the spirituality that mysteriously directs the magazine.

"The magazine project has a life of its own," I explain. "I just simply follow." I think she understands the gist – that God is a part of it.

Then she shares with me her spirituality, in bits and pieces.

"I use my stomach to read situations," she informs me. "If it doesn't feel good, I know something is wrong."

"Really, you use your stomach?" I question. "That's fascinating," I respond, not knowing quite what to make of Priscilla.

"Hey…let's read our horoscopes," she says, grabbing the newspaper off the table. "Maybe it says something about the magazine. You know my spiritual director and her friends predicted you would come with a magazine idea," Priscilla says, as excited as a little kid. "Oh, here, it says, 'Your creativity and time spent over the last six months will impress a group of most prestigious people.' See…that must mean the magazine."

"It must?"

"Next time you visit, I'll arrange for you to meet my spiritual director," suggests Pricilla. "She can reach very high levels."

What does she mean? Why do I need high levels when I have God?

"Oh? And what does she charge?" I ask.

"She's very expensive but really worth it…about one hundred and sixty dollars an hour."

I return home and wait about a week, until she's

actually ready to sit down and write – which takes her another good three or four days. At last, she calls, to let me know she's finished.

"Great," I say. "Fax it to me. So, did you get the feeling of inspiration as you were doing this?"

Priscilla has a hard time answering the question.

"Well, no," she finally says.

"Did you feel like you were being moved...like it was flowing?"

"Everybody feels that way when they write," Priscilla responds.

When I receive the fax, the next day, I read it and overall, my first take is – she's a good writer, but this isn't what it's supposed to be. This feels very sensational and confusing.

"You did a beautiful job," I say so as not to discourage her.

I remind myself to be patient. It will evolve like most magazines. Creating takes time.

Chapter 17

Obstacles in the Attic

*As I did with Mitchell, I painfully take another divine dive
towards the truth about my relationship with Ben. I reflect
back on Mitchell's question, "Do you love Ben?" The truth
rings through, so strong and clear, that it stays with me for
several weeks. My words, "No, I don't, and I don't plan on being married to him the rest of my life," are so powerful that I
can't question my decision anymore. I take a serious pledge to
stay away from Mitchell and to focus on resolving my problems at home.*

*Putting pen to paper, I feel peace coming to me as I record
my thoughts and feelings daily in my journal. It helps me
gain greater clarity, as I approach the next round of turbulence
– this time one that I'm responsible for creating. It's bother-
some to hear Ben say, "I love you." I cringe at being a victim
of his love. I can't tell him the same. I can't love him the way
I did before – unconditionally. I yearn for a true connection. I
take the writing exercise to task in the form of a letter. It hurts
him as he reads my words, "I've lost my love for you." I let
him down easy and continue to explain, "...but I'm willing
to start over in a new direction – as friends first." The friend
angle backfires immediately. Ben takes a nosedive, instead of a
divine dive, into depression and overloads on Prozac.*

As weeks pass, Ben pulls himself together. He's ready to make amends – to say he's sorry. He arranges a special evening to dine out and surprises me with a dozen red roses – a ritual from our past that includes the usual empty promises. We sit at a table for two, surrounded by several tables of couples, hardly making for a private setting.

"Go ahead," he says. "Order yourself a glass of wine. It won't bother me. It's okay." So I do. Ben has no idea what he's walking into, nor does *Linda*. He starts out by saying, "I'm sorry for all the things I've done to hurt you," and tells me about the changes he wants to make.

One glass of wine and minutes later, something ugly inside takes over and *boom* – serpent *Linda* re-enters me with mean and nasty words flying out of her mouth. *It doesn't matter what he says. I want to hurt him she thinks.*

Another whoosh of emotions rise up to the surface, chest level, and before embarrassing myself, I flee the restaurant. I wait in the car for him to come out – no Ben. Then I circle the block a few times and spot him walking down a side street. He shushes me away and shows up at home hours later by cab.

Clearly, I'm at fault. It's my mistake, not *Linda's*, for being too kind in my letter. For losing my grip with truth and leading Ben into thinking we can start over with our relationship. *Linda* is not ready to accept his amends because it's not safe to be in his circle – it never was. It's an utter threat and a roadblock towards my survival.

Broken, weak, and not ready for reconciliation, I fear forgiving because opening my heart is another invitation to be hurt again. I already forgave and forgot easily, several times over. My heart turned to stone because the relationship never

restored itself enough to withstand the next jab. A taste of
love from God through Mitchell has given me the ability to
compare and contrast. It's the only lifeline that holds me from
falling back into the hellhole of Ben's alcoholism.

Obviously, my marriage is beyond repair, it's too late,
and my love's wrung dry. I wish someone with wisdom
would explain to me what my *mystical self* already knows.

"Detach from the circle of evil. Get out of harm's way to
begin the process of forgiveness. To forgive is to heal and to
heal is to forgive."

I'm willing to take the risk of being alone the rest of my
life, to fully forgive, to free my soul from the bondage of
anger and resentment, and to heal.

I take the first step forward by calling a divorce attorney.

The magazine prospectus never does evolve as I'd like
it to because Priscilla takes on an *"I-am-not-changing-this"*
attitude. As far as she's concerned, it's final – done. I can
tell that, unlike me, her heart is not in this project. She
becomes edgy, juggling several projects while searching
for employment.

With great success, I line up meetings with directors
of magazine development from the top four publishing
companies. I have six weeks to fine-tune the project and
to develop presentation boards that clearly focus on the
true intent of the magazine, regardless of the prospectus.
During that time, Priscilla's black Labrador of sixteen
years passes away and she turns remorseful for a couple
of weeks. Now both of us, frazzled with family dysfunction, share our woes as girlfriends do. Priscilla tells me
about her connection with the animal-spirit world. "I saw
my dog's spirit in the house yesterday and my mother

did, too." Again, she reiterates her spiritual director's prediction that I'm "the one coming from the Midwest with the magazine idea."

Around the same time, Dr. Reynolds's manager, Alan, and I agree to a meeting in the Chicago Loop where they broadcast live for the week. We review the prospectus together.

A few days later, Alan calls.

"Dr. Reynolds and I have concerns about your editor," he says. "We don't like the way this is written and think we can get you someone better."

At this point, derailing my project to take time-out to teach someone else the concepts are big steps backwards. Plus, *Linda's* concerned. Using their editor is a loss of control. It could tip the editorial balance far too much in Dr. Reynolds favor, causing the magazine to lose its focus. The people in New York are still asking, "Who's Dr. Reynolds?" – which means her name isn't as important as I once thought. The big question is – does Dr. Reynolds want to continue to ride *my* train?

One morning, a screensaver with a repeat pattern of red hearts that say, "I Love Dr. Reynolds," pops up on my computer. I'm shocked. I really don't know what to make of it and I'm frightened about opening anything in case it contains a virus. I show it to Ben that evening.

"Well, click on the folder underneath and see what it says," he suggests. Inside a message pops up saying, "I really like your idea about a magazine with Dr. Reynolds."

"Someone hacked you!" Ben shouts.

"You did this!" I say.

"I promise. It wasn't me. Really, I didn't do it," he pleads emphatically.

It's bewildering.

"Whoever the hacker is, they rearranged my documents," I say. "Look, it was done at 4 a.m., while we were asleep." *By this time, I'm now doubly appalled and feeling quite violated.*

I'm convinced it was Ben. He's capable of anything to throw me off course – he's a technology genius. And, as crazy as Ben's hacking and Priscilla's bizarre psychics and horoscopes, I consider the hacking incident to be a sign. I decide there's no better time than now to take Advice forward to publishers. I call to confirm our meetings.

Chapter 18

Another Staircase

"I've accepted a position to develop a magazine idea for a publisher," Priscilla announces while sitting at the cafe table in her stark-white kitchen. "The publisher even agreed to have a limo driver take me to and from work every day because it's not a safe commute."

"Will you still have time to work on *Advice*?" I ask, partly happy for her but mostly worried she's going to bail on my project. She shrugs her shoulders and wrinkles her nose. "We'll have to see how it goes," she says.

Our first appointment is with our choice publisher, Gold Publishing Inc. Heading towards Broadway and Seventh, we pass a couple of palm reader shops.

"Why don't we get our palms read?" Priscilla suggests. "How about tomorrow, when we're done with our meetings?"

"That sounds like fun," *Linda* replies.

I'm very naive and not in tune with the powers that control souls like Priscilla. Her mentality takes me back to a time when I first discovered 'spirit world'.

I say out loud, "You know, when I lived in San Francisco, I had an encounter with a ghost..." and from there on, *Linda* finishes telling her tale about the neon blue ghost who shared my bed.

"Well...I had the image of a gargoyle shaking me out of my sleep," Pricilla adds and then clarifies. "It was after I divorced my first husband and was living alone."

We arrive at Four Times Square and ride the elevator up to the 38th floor. We find ourselves stepping out and into an unusually quiet, maple-paneled lobby, where we wait nervously. Coming from behind the paneled walls, Amy Vogel greets us. She's a tall thin woman with soft blond hair, cut in a bob. She signals us to follow her, as she gracefully tip-toes us back to her office. It's so quiet. You'd think a baby was sleeping.

"The goal is emotional well-being," I say holding up the first board. "That's the theme of the magazine." Then I take Amy through the personal growth market and finish with a passion that seems to burst from my center, "It's all about personal responsibility...that's the mission of the magazine."

Amy is totally enthralled and then redirects her attention to Pricilla.

"Well...we tried to develop a couple of covers but they didn't *feel* right," explains Pricilla. "Is it okay if I read the introduction and a few departments?"

"Sure, that sounds great," Amy says.

It's pleasant to listen to Pricilla read her lovely work but I inwardly *cringe* at the parts that don't fit – *the parts that need to evolve.*

"I can see the start of something great," Amy concludes. "Priscilla, would you mind shaping the editorial a bit more? I'd like you both to come back and meet with senior management."

Next, it's a 1:30 p.m. meeting with Matthew Doyle at Magazine Enterprises. He brings in a junior level person and we perform the exact routine from a few hours ago. They both love it.

"We'd like you to come back for a second round." Matt says.

After leaving the building, I'm ecstatic but Priscilla isn't quite the same.

While walking down Broadway, she puts her hand on her stomach. "I don't have a good feeling about this," she says. "I'm very uncomfortable my signature isn't on the confidentiality agreement at Magazine Enterprises."

"Oh...don't worry," I assure her. "I consider signatures on confidentiality agreements more *uncomfortable* than not."

At the end of the day, I call my mother with a blow-by-blow description of the meetings from a hotel that overlooks Central Park at 56th and Seventh.

"And we're going to have our palms read tomorrow," I mention lightheartedly, as we end our conversation.

"Please don't go," my mother blurts out.

I'm puzzled.

"Oh, Mom...it's not a big deal," I laugh.

"Please! Just don't go!" she begs.

Troubled by fear in her voice, I give in. "Okay, I won't."

By this time, I've learned to trust my mother's wisdom, which is far greater than my own.

The next day we have two meetings that don't go as well, and we never do get around to having our palms read. Priscilla needs to be home before her kids return from day camp. I need to get to the airport to catch my flight back. The cab driver first drops Priscilla off and before she gets out, I give her a hug and a prayer – *The Serenity Prayer.* I don't know why I'm compelled to give her the copy. I laminated several of them and stuffed a few in my wallet before coming to New York. After I hand it to Priscilla and she reads it, an extremely embarrassed look comes over her porcelain-white face, turning it red.

"Oh, thanks," Priscilla sheepishly replies, as she slides out the cab, curbside.

Normally, I load my duffle bag full of reading material – mainly self-help and inspirational books that have kept me in balance for almost a full year. With my head still spinning from the trip and more absent-minded than usual, I forget my books as Ben and I head to the yacht club for the weekend.

The next morning we are up early, swimming with the kids at the pool. I stroll back to the boat to check the dogs and grab juice packs. It bothers me that I don't have anything to read and try shrugging it off. About halfway down the long dock, a man is sitting in his beach chair with a crate in front of him. When I approach closer and squint to look down, I can see, oddly enough, that the crate is full of books.

"Excuse me sir, but out of curiosity, what are you doing with all these books?"

"They're irregulars," he says. "I operate a printing press for a publisher and these are irregulars. I'm giving them away because we can't sell them. Go ahead and take whatever you want."

"Really?"

By this time, my head is in the crate searching through some twenty or more books. I stop when I find one book with the word 'community' in the title; it takes me back to the meeting with Amy. I can hear her say, "A sense of community is the connection needed to survive."

"This one looks really interesting," I say as I thumb through its hundreds of pages.

"Go ahead. You can have it," he says.

"Really? Thanks!" I say in amazement while walking towards the boat to quiet our two barking dogs.

It's an odd book – very spiritual and religious at the same time. It makes me uncomfortable at first, because I don't want to read anything religious. For the last couple of years, I've been trying to figure out where I belong. Though I was born Catholic, one year, I'm Lutheran and another year, Protestant. My kids are in a parochial Lutheran school but I go to the First Presbyterian Church. What's most important is that I pray and connect directly to God by saying the 'Our Father.'

Instead of starting at the beginning of the book, I go directly to the chapter on marriage. I'm still trying to decide if and when to file for a divorce. It's as if the author is talking directly to me; telling me what I'm doing wrong and what I'm doing right in my life. He's teaching me how to follow my journey and God through inner guidance. I can't put the book down.

I read on to learn that true partnership has to be in support of your life purpose. Ben can't see the benefits of sharing at this level or even of having a spiritual purpose. He thinks I'm wasting my time. He believes I should get a real job and make real money the way I used to do. I can't. No more steps backwards.

The rest of the summer is easy as my mind is clearer with more objectivity in making decisions. I step outside Ben's chaotic circle and never again do I doubt my gut. The wisdom in my body sharpens with every negative action Ben creates. I feel similar to the way Priscilla does when she holds her stomach and says, "Oh, that doesn't feel right," or "I get a bad feeling." I get a vibration – a warning – that rattles in the middle of my stomach. It's very odd.

It's also very odd finding that book on the dock, too. It comes when I need it the most to help piece my life together. It gives me certainty, strength, and wisdom for a purpose much greater than me.

Chapter 19

Between Rafters

By the close of the summer, Ben emotionally bottoms out.

"I want what you have," he begs.

He stands in front of me, a broken man with hazy sore eyes, witnessing God working in my life – carrying me 'above' my worst nightmare. I'm no longer a confused victim or an angry child. His pain is not my pain. The cycle is broken. I sit outside his circle and carry my children with me. We are safe.

"Either we split up or you come with me and find your spirituality," I say with unwavering conviction.

"Okay, I'll come. I want to go," Ben cries out as he breaks down.

Elma, my other spiritual mother, returns to help me with the kids and daily chores.

"Elma…What's it like when the Holy Spirit moves you? You know – how does it feel? Is it so strong that you can't help but go in a particular direction? Is it like a force with great certainty?"

"Yes, honey. That's right," Elma says. "That's how it feels. You got it Daughter."

The next afternoon, I'm buzzing with energy from the

excitement of adding colorful visuals to my boards. Elma catches me with her Godly deep-brown eyes before I scoot down to my basement office.

"You better be careful of those men in New York," she says surprising me.

I act innocent. "What men?"

"The men who want you," she replies.

Is Elma psychic and close to Jesus at the same time? I wonder. My real mother warned me of psychics, but I know Elma is good. Can psychics be good?

"God shows me things and I'm careful when to share," Elma explains.

I test her – "So who are these men?" She describes their intentions and what they look like.

"One is lurking and wants to break up your marriage. He's tall and thin. The other is lusting in his heart. He's broad built."

How interesting. She's right. I pay attention to the warning and consider it God's way to keep me focused on the magazine – no outside distractions.

I decide to accept Priscilla's kind offer to stay at her place, where I feel safe from anyone lurking or lusting. She and I schedule a manicure before getting down to business. While walking to the salon, I share with her my awakening story and the book on the dock.

"You better be very careful what you read," Priscilla warns.

I don't understand her caution. Then, I hear *Linda's* little voice. *Don't share any more with her, she warns.*

Then Alan calls to tell us Dr. Reynolds wants out and he's no longer her manager.

It's an unfortunate sudden turn of events. We write Dr. Reynolds out while diligently cleaning up our work at the computer in Pricilla's spare bedroom. Interestingly enough, taking Dr. Reynolds out lightens the tone of the magazine. Priscilla chatters to herself, while I take a break lying on the bed looking up at the ceiling. I listen to her glimmers of inspiration as she fine-tunes the prospectus. She seems lighter, too, and it sounds like she's grasping the concept. Finally, she gets that it's a magazine on emotional well-being by adding a few new departments that are from the inside out.

"That's great. That's great," I say. "I love it. That's really good. You're on the right path. Keep going." I suggest adding more inspiration to the edit mix. She ignores me.

I print out a back-up copy of the document for a final check. We mark up the changes on the hard copy and then make the corrections on Word Document. Great! We're finished. When making the very last change, my sleeve hits the delete button. I lose the entire document.

"No problem," I say, "I'm familiar with sassy computers. I have one at home." I go to Edit and glide the curser to Undo Typing. Everything should come back. Nothing comes back. The screen stays blank. The document is completely erased from Priscilla's computer. It's gone. We don't have a back-up disk, either. It's not anywhere on her computer. We both look at each other in shock.

First, I smile.

Then, Priscilla smiles.

"We're not supposed to leave a copy!" we laugh and say in unison.

The next morning we're up early, dressed in our best suits with polished nails, rehearsing before going to

Magazine Enterprises.

"There's something that really bothers me when you present," Priscilla says.

"Oh what is it?"

"You say the word 'I' all the time and we're a team. We're together in this and you should say 'we,'" she replies, clearly rattled.

As she speaks, I feel her negative vibration hit the center of my stomach.

"Something's not right here," *Linda* whispers quietly in my ear. "She's really hung up on the 'we.'"

"I've worked on *Advice* for almost two years," I say kindly. "I've done most of the work myself. You've only been working on it for a few months."

"And hardly, at that," *Linda* whispers, a second time.

"I'd like an equal share in all this," Priscilla says. "We should be a team. We need to give off a sense that we're together."

I know the importance of 'we' in business – but I'm not in agreement with her wanting an equal share.

Chapter 20

Bell Tower

We sit at the beautiful, finely crafted cherry-wood conference table with lustrous paneled walls surrounding us. We're ready to begin. Glen Forester, the president of Magazine Enterprises, enters the office. He's a man in his seventies. It's an honor to meet him. He was the editor-in-chief of one the oldest women's service magazines for over a decade. I remember hearing his voice over P.A. systems in grocery stores, doling out cooking tips and home remedies.

I sit at one end and Mr. Forester, the opposite. Priscilla sits in the middle across from the company's editorial director and Matt.

"People and their problems," is my opening line as I hold up a board with about twenty colorful magazine covers reduced to fit. Each cover highlights a different celebrity who has dealt with adversity or undergone some kind of transformation. I'm nervous and stumble over the word 'people.' As soon as I do, a vision appears in front of me. The vision isn't in my minds eye – it's outside of me. It appears about two feet away giving me a panoramic view of images unfolding as on a sixty-inch TV screen. It feels like I'm out of sync with time.

The scene takes place in a church. I see three tall stained-glass windows in the background. I see several rows of pews. The church is not full. It's the middle of the week when people come to light candles and say confession. There are three women with gray curly hair kneeling in separate pews, praying.

As quick as the vision comes, a tremendous sensation enters from the top of my head, travels the length of my body, filling every inch of my being. It's love running through my entire body. The feeling is powerful. That's God. God is love. God is with me.

Then I return. I'm back in time. I'm back in the room. Then something tickles me and lifts my whole body up. I want to say, "Ooh," because it feels good, but I don't really say anything. I look at everybody. I can see they're looking at me the same as when I left. Yes. Time did stand still. I regain my composure. I'm back into my presentation and it just flows out of me. I'm singing it. I sing it like a bird – just beautiful.

It's Priscilla's turn. She's really nervous about presenting the material. It's a dilemma for her – figuring out how to present. She's a beautiful writer. She really does have a way with words.

"Why don't you read it," I had said to her earlier. "If that's what makes you comfortable, then that's the way you should present it."

She uses very simple boards – using the words food, health, fashion and beauty – to make her point.

It's not going very smoothly. Trying to read and hold up boards at the same time isn't working for Priscilla. I watch Mr. Forester listen to her read as he closes his eyes. I don't think he's falling asleep. I think he's trying to visualize the magazine. I watch him put his hands on his head and rub his temples like it's disturbing or confusing. After Priscilla finishes, Mr. Forester asks a few questions about the spirituality in the magazine.

"Oh, yes, it's an underlying current throughout," Priscilla says.

Mr. Forester shifts his focus. I see imaginary bells and whistles going off in his mind. He rapidly fires questions directly at me about the market and the magazine. It's not me and it's not *Linda* answering his questions. If there's ever a time to believe in the Holy Spirit, spirit guides, higher-self, many masters, or whatever one wants to call it – it's this time. It's too perfect. It just flows too beautifully. Still infused with love, a power greater than me speaks.

Between all the questions, I can't help but notice the priceless look on Matt's face. His big blue eyes register fear and amazement all at once.

"The goal is to attain emotional well-being," I tell Mr. Forester. "People going through hardship or adversity have other problems. Stress takes a toll on our looks causing premature aging, hair loss, weight loss, weight gain, and so many other conditions – Truly, there is a mind/body connection."

My final words deliver closure.

"Women need to connect with a magazine that can help them along the way."

It hits Mr. Forester really big. He gets it.

"I want to test this on the newsstand," he says.

I sneak in a call to Mitchell from Priscilla's house just hours later.

"Mr. Forester wants to test *Advice* on the newsstand," I

say excitedly, giving Mitchell the privilege of being the first to hear my news.

"Congratulations! That's wonderful. Now when do you meet with Gold Publishing?" asks Mitchell.

"Oh, I'm so nervous. We meet with them tomorrow."

"You'll do great. Remember, you're the expert," Mitchell encourages. "That's why they're meeting you. You have nothing to be nervous about," he says, lifting my spirit.

"Thanks. You're right," I say, swallowing my fear. "Do you still want to meet for drinks tomorrow?" I ask openly.

"Yes. Call me when you're done," he responds softly.

The vision of God's love hasn't fully surfaced into the reality of my world. I'm still in shock. I'm still processing. I can't speak it.

It's impossible. My mystical child could not will her eyes to manufacture a vision. It was beyond her creative stretch. The best I can explain about what happened is that the Omnipresence of God's love – located at the heart's center, where the soul flutters – filled me up. His Love brought wholeness to the places where I am broken. Fragmented. And in that brief absence of time, I traveled to where stars twinkle and God's love embraces every inch – yes, every inch of my soul. I touched Heaven – a place we're all from. Then I traveled back, in the fullness, to share the wisdom of healing. I became all three – Riley, Linda and something greater than me.

From this point forward, I lean less on the human elements of life and more directly on God. The annointing of God's love guides my path. I'm strong. I no longer blindly believe, nor do I question or wonder anymore. What I feel is real. God is real.

Life

Life is to live and life is to give
And talents are to use for good if you choose.
Do not pray for easy lives.
Pray to be strong.
Do not pray for tasks equal to your powers.
Pray for powers equal to your tasks –
Then the doing of your work shall be no
Miracle but you shall be a miracle.
Every day you shall wonder at yourself...
At the richness of life which has come
To you by the grace of God.
But everyone needs someone –
Knowing that somewhere someone is thinking of you.

– Anonymous

Chapter 21

Standing Tall

That evening, after a couple of glasses of wine at a Thai restaurant, Priscilla starts to babble. Fear sets in. "I just don't know how I'm going to get through the presentation tomorrow," she says, voicing the same fears that I had earlier.

"It'll be just fine," I say. "Remember, we're the experts."

"Oh, no – you don't understand," she says shrinking even more. "I don't have a good feeling about this." After downing her second glass of wine too easily, Priscilla's insecurities worsen to the point of embarrassment. "I've been in front of these people before," she says with a distorted brow and eyes filling with tears. "They'll try and tear me apart."

Her words slur and by now, Priscilla's drinking wears on me. Her drunkenness triggers memories in my body cells. I flash back to the torment of living with an alcoholic. She reminds me of Ben. Oh, no – not her. I can't help but think – she's an alcoholic, too.

This time, the conference room and table are much larger than the ones at Magazine Enterprises and the atmosphere is more sterile. Just before the room fills, I excuse myself to go to the ladies room. In the stall, I take five deep breaths to calm my nerves and say the *'Our Father.'*

As I return to the conference room, two presidents and two editorial directors from several divisions within the company enter as well. There are four of them and two of us, filling half the seats around the table.

I haven't shared my vision with Priscilla yet. I'm still trying to absorb it. Although I notice she seems much better this morning.

For me, my confidence rides high knowing that an offer is on the table at Magazine Enterprises, and that God's love holds me, Mitchell supports me, and my mother is home taking good care of my children and Ben. Everything is in balance. I breathe calmly. Though sometimes I've had trouble breathing before, this time I feel fine.

After we go through the introductions of who's who, I begin my part. *(Good, I'm not shaking, either.)* Their eyes shine and heads nod up and down, as I flip through my colorful boards so carefully crafted. They're with me – hanging on my every sentence. I share *Advice's* goal of emotional well-being and then present key aspects of the personal growth market which includes spirituality, inspiration, psychotherapy, support groups, and journaling. I give them the facts they crave hearing about.

They don't realize that my guarded secrets are integrated into my beautiful boards: that I'm the target audience; that I'm the victim desperately trying to dodge the cycle of abuse; that I'm really sharing my treasure chest of survival tools; that my passion for the magazine is really channeled anger; that the magazine calmly releases Linda's inferno; that the foundation of Advice – family values and personal responsibility – keep me from having an affair; and that the magazine is

really driven by Riley, Linda, and my mystic child to help save
others. All and all, the invisible spine that I envision holding
the pages of my magazine together really holds my fragile
life together.

Next, Priscilla reads the prospectus while holding up
her boards. The faces in the room get very serious. The
two editors tilt their heads ever so carefully to visualize
while listening to her every word. One man in particular
shakes his head from side to side. I catch his look of disgust as Priscilla sweetly delivers a phrase about 'painting
toenails.' Not a good sign, especially since he's the editorial director. Priscilla's fear is manifesting. Her trusty gut
proves right. I sense silent criticism bubbling up among
the group mid-way through the prospectus.

The onslaught begins.

"You're not daring enough," says a female president.
"This is a breakthrough magazine concept. You should be
more out there."

Out there...where? New Age? Is that what she means?

Next, the editorial director turns his attention to Priscilla. "What Riley has just presented and what you wrote
don't fit together," he says. "I want to hear more life-con-
necting...you know...more heartwarming stories. I want
to hear about taking time out of your day to go shoot
hoops with your kids."

All along, I knew the magazine wasn't quite there. My at-
titude was – it will evolve. I practiced keeping the focus on
myself, instead of trying to control Priscilla. "To change the
things I can...." was the wisdom I used from The Serenity
Prayer. It was frustrating. Priscilla wasn't tweaking Advice
according to any of my suggestions, so I put my ideas in the
market presentation. That's why we didn't match up. Like

the 'dance of life'...when one changes, the other must follow.
Priscilla didn't follow.

"What are you looking for, Riley?" a top-level executive boldly inquires shifting the conversation to business.

"Well...I just want the magazine tested on the newsstand."

"No, no, no. I mean, what's your take?" he asks with a cold stare and lines crinkled across his forehead.

Priscilla answers quickly, "Riley's the publisher and I'm the editor."

"Whose idea is it?" he asks directing the question back to me.

"It's my idea," I answer. "I'm the target audience," I say, as if removing my mask.

Priscilla's plan of using 'we' begins to dissolve.

I continue telling my story. "After researching the magazine's audience, I sat down in front of my computer and an overwhelming feeling came – I couldn't stop writing. My fingers barely kept up," I say reliving my experience.

From that point, the discussion opens to the topic of spirituality and they seem to confuse it with New Age thinking. I bring the conversation back to the magazine. "This magazine is really about personal responsibility," I say with great passion. "It's about life!" Amy and the editorial director both smile in agreement.

Then the editorial director reaches out to shake my hand. "I look forward to working with you," he says with a glint in his eyes.

"I look forward to working with you, too," I respond.

Priscilla and I thank everyone, leave the conference room, and walk to the lobby.

"Wow, that went really well," I say as we ride down in

the elevator. I can't help but reflect back to the image of
the editorial director shaking my hand, as if it's a
done deal.

"Well, I don't have a good feeling," says Priscilla.

"Oh really? Seems like they want to do this. That's good
enough for me," I say, blocking her negativity.

Back at Priscilla's apartment I call Mitchell.

"Priscilla and I have plans to go to the Met. Can you
meet me afterwards?

"That only gives us a half hour before you'll have to
leave to make your flight."

"Oh, I didn't realize."

"You'll be back. You'll be back several times for the
magazine."

"Yes, you're right. I will."

*This is too much; too nerve-wracking; too awkward. I want
so much to be with him but I know it's wrong. Nothing can
come of this, as long as we're both married. But the ache never
goes away. The best I can do is to use my ache as my measure
of wellness. When I feel the pain go deep in my heart, I know
I'm healing through layers of protection built-up from my relationship with my father and Ben. The continual pattern of loving and letting go helps free the blockage. Then God whispers,
"Be still, my dear. Accept the simplicity of this love so rare. A
mystic life is what I share."*

Priscilla and I find a table under the beautiful atrium.
With a fresh shrimp salad and a side of French bread
set before us, we toast to our success with crystal glasses
filled with fizzy spring water.

"You won't believe what happened," I say to Priscilla.
"Remember at Magazine Enterprises when I stumbled

over the word 'people'?" I then tell her about the vision
of the women praying in the church and God's love.

She quickly says, "I asked my mother to pray. It must
have been my mother's prayers."

*I'm sure she's right. Prayers do connect us to God's love and
guidance but it's the tone in her voice that bothers me. There it
is again. I pick up on her subtle attitude – the one that dispels
God's power. I sensed it before. Whenever I shared my light
– the inspiration for the magazine, my spiritual awakening
or when I gave her The Serenity Prayer – I sensed her negative attitude come through. Contrary to my beliefs, Priscilla
manifested a gargoyle, followed horoscopes and was drawn to
psychics and palm readers. She even tried pulling me in.*

At Priscilla's brownstone before catching my flight
home, we discuss retrieving the lost document.

"I'll scan the hard copy onto a disk and clean up my
part before sending it out," I say.

Next, I look at Priscilla and as I speak I feel completely
exhausted. "You know, my boards are really heavy," I say,
rubbing my neck. "I'm sure I'll be back. You hold on to
them. I'm so tired...I just don't have the energy to carry
them back." So I leave my boards with her – my only set.

Priscilla helps me with my bags to the curb, where the
cab waits. I give her a warm hug and wave good-bye from
the cab, never thinking that this will be our last embrace.

Chapter 22

Be Still, My Dear

I'm exhausted from the trip. The next day, I take several short naps and crash early that evening after tucking the kids in. Ben cooperates and scans the document at his office. According to plan, I try cleaning it up. It just isn't flowing. I'm aggravated with it and have no patience.

"Would you mind cleaning up your part?" I ask Priscilla. "I'll send it to you by express mail. You'll have it by tomorrow. I'm just really having a hard time. I'm not settled and just can't do it right now."

"No problem," says Priscilla.

As soon as the disk arrives in her hands, something magically evil transpires. Priscilla is granted the illusion of power.

"I'm feeling very uncomfortable. I would like a contract entitling me to a portion of the magazine," she demands over the phone. "And I'm not sending the work to the publishers until you do."

"I'll get something to you by the end of the week," I say. "I promise."

"The quality of my relationships determines the quality of my life," says Marshall Summers. At one level, I'm awake enough to know the signs of an alcoholic but I never took it a

step further in recognizing the signs of an abusive personality.
Underneath alcoholism, drug abuse, or any sort of addictive
behavior, lay patterns of abuse. The alcohol, drugs or any
other addictions are simply symptoms. Between my upbringing
and the publishing culture, what appeared normal, in real-
ity, wasn't. Anyway, I'm caught in another unhealthy cycle
because I'm missing signs at the outset about Priscilla.

I can't get through to her for a good hour. I want to
keep Priscilla in the loop. As I listen to the busy signal, it
occurs to me...she's talking to her spiritual director, who's
really a psychic. That's why the line is tied up for so long.
I visualize the psychic channeling and feeding her information. Control and manipulation is another 'sign.'

Finally, I get through. I'm absolutely right!

"Your name can't be on the title," I tell her. "I already
filed and we'd have to incorporate as a company." I continue to update her on my progress. "I'm working on the
contract and you'll have it by the end of the week."

Then Priscilla shifts her tone to *girlfriend* style. "When
I was on the phone with my spiritual director, she said
there will be a thirty-six-hour waiting period."

Oh, brother. I'm not falling for this *con*, anymore.
Priscilla's adviser is not a spiritual director. There's nothing sacred about her.

Priscilla continues, "She tells me something will happen within a thirty-six-hour waiting period but doesn't
know what is."

I hang up and think...*yeah right, a thirty-six-hour*
waiting period...funny how they don't know what happens in
between. Well, I know why they don't know. It's me they can't
figure out. It's my part, because God is blocking them.

What is important is to be alert and to understand the next moves. I know how it works. When one thing happens, the rest falls into place. I know what to do. I must be still and wait until I make contact with Matt at Magazine Enterprises.

What bothers me most is the lack of faith people have. Priscilla has little faith and depends on a channeler to get her though this difficult time. I felt intrigued, at first, and saw the power in predicting events. It has proved to be very useless. Now she is using the channeling against me. I've been praying for her. She mentioned a thirty-six-hour waiting period and something in the middle that is missing. Ha! It's me maneuvering through all this mess. God is guiding me and that is exactly why the channeler is missing this piece because it's God's will. I strongly believe something will come of this. I must stay on course and stay clean.

Chapter 23

Cleaning Closets

From this point, the clock is ticking (if I'm to believe Priscilla).

Finally, I break the news to Priscilla on Saturday morning.

"Gold Publishing is passing because the editorial focus wasn't clear."

Priscilla's speechless and then hangs up.

Emotionally, I don't falter. Instead, I visualize a net, stretched out mid-air, that breaks my fall and an unusual calmness penetrates my center.

"Yes, when one door closes, another opens," I say to Ben.

"What a cliché," remarks Ben. "Does that mean you're not going to look for another job?"

"Of course…if I have to," I say firmly. "But Magazine Enterprises is still interested."

Billy, Lizzie, and Michele are dressed in their Sunday best, waiting with me in the car for Ben to lock up. He pops his head around the screen door and points to the phone in his hand.

"It's Priscilla on the phone," he calls out.

"I can't talk to her right now," I shout back. "Just tell

her we're going to church and I'll call her when we get back."

That morning, the sermon is about battling the unseen forces and the importance of relying on God. I can't help but notice the message is aimed directly at me. Down on my knees, I pray even more intensely in silent conversation, asking for strength and guidance on the magazine.

I hope for Priscilla's heart to turn humble, between the hours that pass. I hope her illusion of power dissipates. Maybe she'll be calm, more peaceful today. Maybe she's thought things over and will be reasonable, so we can work together.

As soon as Priscilla gets on the phone, the opposite is true. There is no peace. She's still nasty and demanding.

Time expires – thirty-six hours have passed and so has her power.

Suddenly, *Linda's* and *my mystical child* soul ignite together and razor-sharp words rapidly fly out of our mouth. "You know what? I've been praying for you and you are going the wrong way. I don't want to have anything to do with you. I'm done with you. We're done. I don't care if I have to start all over again. I'll start from scratch. We're done," both *Linda* and I announce with unwavering conviction.

Priscilla doesn't respond. Instead, she hands the phone to her husband.

"Well...I guess you two are done," he calmly says.

"Yes we are and I'll put that in writing," I calmly reply back.

Yes, I'd rather start over. Start from scratch. I'd rather run the risk of losing Magazine Enterprises, than have Priscilla as the editor of Advice. She's anything but emotionally and spiritually healthy. All day Saturday, I felt her negative energy was incredibly heavy, almost paralyzing and harmfully binding.

I celebrate life as a 'victim-no-more.' I look for a direction that has flow; that has freedom. I completely let go. I give up all thinking with the rational mind, with no strategy and no motive directing me. My prayers open me up, so my soul can see. I run for the light.

Now, everything is wiped away. I have nothing. I'm empty. I assume, without Priscilla, my chances at Magazine Enterprises are gone. But it feels good when I hang up. I'm relieved to be rid of the evil threatening my magazine and me. She was a liability. Priscilla's strange breed of spirituality would have utterly destroyed the true intentions of the magazine.

Still seeing with spiritual eyes open, I'm certain the angels have won this battle. I call my mother to celebrate my 'letting go.'

"I fired Priscilla!" I exclaim.

"You did?" she asks. "Well, I'm so proud of you. Let me read something interesting to you," Mom says excitedly. "I just so happen to be studying this in my bible study this week." We giggle together knowing we're about to have one of those moments – when God uses my mother to affirm me. "Listen..." she says.

Isaiah 8: 19,20.

And when they say to you, "Seek those who are mediums and wizards, who whisper and mutter," should not a people seek their God? Should they seek the dead on behalf of the living? To the law and to the testimony! If they do not speak according to this word it is because there is no light in them.

Monday morning comes and I take a deep breath to work

up my nerve before calling Matt. This time, I don't bother saying a prayer. I figure it's already over. I let go.

"Well, I've lost my editor," I say bracing for his rejection.

"Oh, no big deal...editors are a dime a dozen," Matt says. "It's the concept we like."

I'm silent, not believing my ears.

"Well...the concept is *yours*...right?" asks Matt.

"Well, of course, it's mine," I answer, still in shock. "But I'll need an editor."

"Okay...I'll talk to Mr. Forester and see what we can do," he says.

I'm determined to get my magazine presentation boards back. The only way I feel comfortable doing this is to go through Priscilla's husband. So I call him at work and make arrangements for shipping them back. During the wait, tremendous evil looms in and around me. The attacks start all over again. The vibration is so intense and powerful it feels like I'm standing too close to the edge of a track as a train blows through. That's the unmistakable force of evil and don't let anyone kid you, it's real.

My other spiritual mother arrives Wednesday morning to help me with the laundry while the kids are at school. *Linda* waits eagerly for Elma to hang up her coat and put on her slippers before telling her.

"Well...I did it," says *Linda*. "I got rid of Priscilla."

"Honey...I didn't want to tell you...but that woman was planning on stealing your magazine," says Elma in her matter-of-fact voice.

"What do you mean?" I ask, puzzled.

"I mean that woman wanted the whole thing," she

says, raising her right eyebrow with light shining through both eyes. "You be careful of her. I see her at the copy machine. I see her making copies of everything."

Finally, my boards arrive by the end of the week. I'm relieved. The *evil* lifts. It goes away. It just all goes away.

Chapter 24

My 40's
Dream Awakening

It's 4:00 A.M.
We yell at the top of our lungs, "We love you, Linda." I see
flames bellow from her mouth. Suddenly, a rush of energy
swirls up from within and pulls me out of my sleep.

I lay there stunned. A memory quickly floods my mind from the night before as I hear his words and feel him holding my face.

"You're my angel," whispers Mitchell. Streams of gold rays flow from his eyes into mine. From the corner of my eye, I see the valet swing my car around to the front door of Stephanie's Restaurant. I get in and wave goodbye to Mitchell through the front window while I pull onto Fullerton Avenue.

Six inches of new snow has accumulated over the last three hours and "On Angels Wings," plays as it guides me through fresh tracks of snow – to begin my life once more.

Epilogue

My Dream House

It's taken five long years of writing this book to fully release the pain of all that I've experienced. The result has freed me from my victim mentality and has given me insight into healthy relationships. It has also led me to find compassion and forgiveness within myself and towards others – where true freedom resides.

House of Healing

Maybe you noticed the levels of emotional healing corresponding with the rooms in Linda's house through her various stages of personal growth.

The first level, in the basement, originates from childhood and family issues passed down from generation to generation. It's the beginning stage of waking to one's spiritual self. It's the reclaiming of a foundation lost or never fully formed as far back as childhood.

Next, the second level, which takes place on the main floor, is the purification stage. During the cleansing, most people are in intense emotional pain causing the heart/soul to crack open to an awareness of 'spirit world' and God.

Shortly after my Linda dream, another one came that

*sounds silly, but was extremely symbolic. It was about releas-
ing a twenty pound bowel movement too big to flush down the
toilet. My whole family and relatives were visiting and gath-
ered in the kitchen and dining room. I was embarrassed. I was
stuck in the bathroom not knowing what to do. My sister came
in to see if I was okay and then she snuck me down the hall
so I could empty it out in the garbage can in the alley. This
dream was about all the stuff passed down from generation
to generation and, symbolically, was a freeing of my family
issues around alcohol abuse.*

*Significant life changing dreams usually come in threes.
Of course, after the second dream, came a third, where I saw
myself under a glass casket, as it represented the part in me
that died. It was a frightful dream. This is the third form of
healing which is a combination of emotional and inner healing that integrates the fragmented personality into one. As I
went through the third level, I did not dare walk alone. I was
in spiritual direction. It means having to face the parts we
don't like about ourselves, admit our faults and make changes.
I worked intensely, but, I must admit, once in a while Linda
still comes out.*

*Remember, the emotional levels of healing repeat themselves
each time at higher levels and vibrations throughout life.
It is truly about climbing the spiral staircase the journey
towards joy.*

The Wisdom of Emotion

*The mind-body naturally achieves balance and well-being
through the wisdom gained in understanding meanings and
measures of emotion. The wise ones who practiced ancient
Chinese medicine – the ying and the yang of finding balance
within – know that emotions cause mental and physical dis-*

*orders. In fact, as I wrote this story I could feel an emotional
vapor escape out of the pores of my body. The unseen residue
would float around for days as it altered my mood and then,
poof, disappeared.*

*Over several years, I have grown to understand that my
choice of relationships and social environment can truly affect
my emotional well-being. Now, it's easier for me to recognize
unhealthy cycles, as I have a clearer understanding of myself.
As long as I stay centered and focused on the higher values
of love, divine truth, and a greater purpose, I'm healthy. I'm
no longer a victim imprisoned behind my own walls. I am
free. Depression, obsessions, and compulsions are symptoms
of negative emotions that constrict or contort the flow of our
emotional and physical bodies. They only serve to help us
measure wellness until they eventually disappear.*

The More You Heal, the More You Feel

*The more you heal, the more you feel. When you start to dispel
negative energies, your body will be more sensitive to other people
and their energies. Remember, the burn in the stomach is about
other people's bad energy. Beware of those who make you feel this
way.*

*The body is a wealth of information that can be used as a
register before the brain can figure something out. The body reads
energy from the memories of past life moments – from this lifetime or from our ancestors' lifetimes – stored and passed down.*

*Go with reading your feelings versus acting on them. They are
here to serve you, not for you to serve them. Discern them carefully and make only wise attachments in life.*

Higher Values Begin with Love

First, let me explain one thing about love. Love does not

belong to the giver or the taker. Love only belongs to God for reasons we'll never know. Love is what heals us. Although most of us confuse love with pain, pain is not love at all. Love is what opens the rooms to our house, our hearts, and our souls. When we open those doors, sometimes there's a surprise waiting – unhealthy emotions screaming to get out –and we have serious work to do.

True love is about friendship and it lasts forever. It is about letting the other person own their own stuff and not getting in their way. It is about having patience for the other to catch up or vice versa or to ride along side-by-side. Love flows through us and around us. It can envelop our whole body. It can lift us up or bring us together. God's love is always glorious but can be painful when taken away by others.

To this very day, I continue to remind myself of the pain that lies in the hearts and souls of all humankind. It is our divine journey of discovery to learn to release that pain through God's love. And only through God's love can we heal. You see, that is the wake-up call knocking on the door of every heart, telling us to open our hearts to drain the pain. The toxic emotional energies deep inside are what cause illnesses of all sorts. It is about looking deeply within. As we heal our emotions, we heal our bodies. It's through God's love that we're able to release the pain pushing up deep from within, desperately needing to come out. It is the bravest of souls who can reflect on their inner selves and not blame others for their pain. It is not anyone's responsibility other than our own to heal our childhood wounds with the help of God's love and understanding.

Nothing but the Truth
In my life, today, the only thing I know for sure is nothing. That's because every day is new. Every day we have to let go

and expect the unexpected. In the world of God, there are no absolutes except pure truth. A deep relationship with God is formed by finding your own truth, and taking the divine dive into your core. We cannot judge others because their reality belongs to them and only them. We must have compassion because suffering is personal. Most people don't intend to hurt others but out of fear they end up hurting the ones who love and care about them.

What you feel belongs to you and no one else. It is guidance given at that moment to help us move along the journey of life. It is about paying attention to something beyond. No one can tell you what you feel or how you feel – only you know that. Sometimes, you can feel what someone else feels when you have both gone through similar situations. You may share a special connection even though you hardly know the person. We are attracted to those who have the same kind of energy, or pain, to help us heal our woundedness. Sometimes, we are attracted to the opposite energy that can help us to stretch and grow from the inside. As you heal, your reality will change because your energy has changed – you have healed.

I eventually left my husband as I gained objectivity about the situation and realized that no matter how much I tried to alter the situation, he'd change at his own pace. I didn't know it was possible to divorce someone you loved. But I understood that the pain on top of pain would never end until I removed myself completely. Once I created a healthier environment for myself and my children, we would begin to have a better future.

I also let go of Mitchell as I discovered the love belonged to God to heal the wounded child within. As I healed, the pain lessened and it really had nothing to do with Mitchell. I discovered that my pain was really from negative emotions absorbed from situations involving criticism, abandonment, physical abuse, embarrassment and guilt— and that I had to find forgiveness within myself and towards others, to ultimately find joy. My most powerful heart healings came, emotionally, through creativity with the magazine and this book, and, spiritually, through Jesus and the Holy Spirit.

Life is a drama of change. Recently, I thought for sure I rid myself of the pain inside only to discover I was still holding onto my fix-it box. I'm what you call a little Miss Fix- It. Being the youngest in my family and having witnessed an abuser in action with all my siblings, I was attracted to fixing abusive men. Now I've learned to throw my fix-it box away completely – well, maybe. The only way I can help others is through sharing my life story so they can fix themselves.

A Greater Purpose

During adverse times, most of us turn towards the light and come closer to God. For me, I swing pretty far and the mystic in me comes alive. The left side of my brain completely shuts down and the right takes over. I'm in tune to the spirit world.

I wasn't prepared for the encounter with my mother's spirit, especially since she had just died two days before. It was her favorite perfume I smelled lingering under my nose that early morning. I knew she was giving a visit but I was too scared to appreciate it. Instead I laid there with the covers over my head pretending I was asleep and hoping for her to go away.

A few weeks later, she came to me in a dream. I felt her presence. When I opened my eyes, her brilliant spirit, the color magenta, filled my bedroom. This time I wasn't scared and it soothed me fast asleep again.

The next morning, I could feel a rumbling inside moving me towards my purpose. In only a few short weeks, I published a

*journal to complement **What You Feel is Real** and began
my career as a coach to help others move forward in positive
directions in their lives.*

*The second dream came a few days before Christmas. My
mother stood behind a door to the Universe. She pried it open a
wee bit and asked if I'd accept the guidance. A powerful force
entered my body and I let it take me. Again, I knew it was
about my purpose. After five years of healing my wounds and
my family, it was time to get this book out.*

Finally the third dream came on Christmas day.

*When my mother had been in the hospital, my sister and I
made a deal with her. We asked if she would come to us in our
dreams and let us know what it was like in heaven.*

*She kept her promise. After she passed away, I dreamt of her
calling me on the phone. I heard her voice. "Kathy," she said,
"It's wonderful here."*

*That night, I crawled under my covers trying to take it all in.
I laid there, feeling the grandness of life. Soon I fell fast asleep,
soothed by my mother's peace and pleased her spirit unlocked
something wonderful inside me like my father's spirit did some
twenty years before. I still feel the grandness of life but this
time, I know guidance is seconds away to aid me with my
purpose. This time, I know we're all connected to our spiritual
family and to God. This time, at forty-seven years of age, I
don't wonder about the person I am to be; instead, I dream
about the person I am.*

Recommended Books

Emotional Well-Being

- Alice D. Domar, Ph.D. and Henry Dreher. *Healing Mind, Healthy Woman*. Henry Holt and Company, 1996.
- Denise Foley, Eileen Nechas, and The Editors of Prevention. *Women's Encyclopedia of Health & Emotional Healing*. Bantam, 1993.
- Daniel Goleman, *Emotional Intelligence*. Bantam Books, 1995.
- George Leonard and Michael Murphy. *The Life We Are Given*. A Jeremy P. Tarcher/Putnam Book, 1995.
- The Institute of Noetic Sciences with William Poole. *The Heart of Healing*. Turner Publishing, Inc., 1993
- Carol Travris. *The Mismeasure of Woman*. Simon & Schuster, 1992.

Inspiration

- Sarah Ban Breathnach. *Simple Abundance*. Warner Books, 1995.
- Jack Canfield & Mark Victor Hansen. *Chicken Soup for the Soul* and *A 2nd Helping of Chicken Soup for the Soul*. Health Communications Inc.1995.
- Dr. Wayne W. Dyer with Marlene Dyer. *A Promise Is a Promise*. Hay House, 1996.
- Betty K Eadie. *Embraced by the Light*. Bantam Book.
- *Forever Remembered*. Compendium Incorporated, Publishing & Communication.

- Shakti Gawain. *Awakening.* Nataraj, 1991.
- Rokelle Lerner. *Affirmations for the Inner Child.* Health Communications, 1990.
- Rokelle Lerner. *Daily Affirmations for Adult Children of Alcoholics.* Health Communications, 1985.

Self-Help

- Les Brown. *Live Your Dreams.* Avon Books, 1992
- Richard Carlson, Ph.D., *Don't Sweat the Small Stuff.* Hyperion, 1997.
- Stephen R. Covey. *The 7Habits of Highly Effective People.* Fireside, 1989, 1994.
- Gavin De Becker. *The Gift of Fear.* Little, Brown and Company, 1997.
- Marcia Germaine Hutchinson, Ed.D. *Transforming Body Image.* The Crossing Press, 1985.
- Loretta LaRoche, *Relax–you may only have a few minutes left.* Villard, 1998.
- Joyce Meyer. *Managing Your Emotions. Instead of your Emotions Managing You!* Harrison House, Inc., 1997.
- Michael Ray and Rochelle Myers. *Creativity in Business.* Doubleday, 1986.
- Anthony Robbins. *Awaken the Giant Within.* A Fireside Book Simon & Schuster, 1991.
- Bernard Selling. *In Your Own Voice.* Hunter House, 1994.
- Dennis Wholey. *The Courage to Change.* Warner Books, 1984.
- Struart Wilde. *The Force and Silent Power.* Hay House, Inc.
- David Wilkerson. *Promises to Live By.* Regal Books, 1972.

Wellness and Recovery

- *Keep It Simple.* Hazelden, 1989.
- *Courage to Change.* Al-Anon Family Group Headquarters, Inc., 1992.
- Melody Beattie. *Codependent No More, Beyond Codependency.* A Hazelden Book, HarperCollins Publishers, 1989.
- Melody Beattie. *Codependent No More, The Language of Letting Go.* A Hazelden Book, HarperCollins Publishers, 1990.
- Janet Geringer Woititz, Ed.D. *Adult Children of Alcoholics.* Health Communication, Inc., 1983.
- Jennifer Louden, *The Woman's Comfort Book and A Little Book of Sensual Comfort.*
- Anne Marie Nuechterlein. *Families of Alcoholics.* Augsburg, 1993.
- Gayle Rosellini and Mark Worden. *Of Course You're Angry.* A Hazelden Book, HarperCollins Publishers, 1985.
- Christiane Northrup, M.D. *Women's Bodies, Women's Wisdom.* Bantam, 1994.
- Joni Arredia, *Muliebrity: Qualities of a Woman.*
- Thomas R. McCabe, Ph.D. *Victims No More.* Hazelden, 1978.
- Robert J. Wicks, *Self-Care for Every Day.* Abbey Press, 1991.
- Neil Clark Warren, *Ph.D. Make Anger Your Ally.* Focus on the Family, 1990.
- Carolynn Hillamn, C.S.W. *Love Your Looks.* Fireside Simon & Schuster, 1996.
- Caroline Myss, Ph.D. *Anatomy of the Spirit.* Harmony Books, 1996.
- Barbara Leahy Shlemon. *Healing the Wounds of Divorce: A Spiritual Guide to Recovery.* Ave Maria Press, 1992.

Relationships/Psychology

- John Gray. *Men are From Mars, Women are From Venus*. HarperCollins.
- John Gray. *Venus in the Bedroom*. HarperCollins.
- Harriet G. Lerner, Ph.D., *The Dance of Intimacy*. Perennial Library, 1989.
- Dean Ornish, M.D. *Love & Survival*. HarperCollins Publishers, 1997.
- Daphne Rose Kingma. *Heart & Soul*. Conari Press, 1995
- Laura Schlessinger. *Ten stupid things women do to mess up their lives*. HarperPerennial, 1994.
- Laura Schlessinger. *How could you do that?!* Harper Collins Publishers, 1996

Psychology/Mythology

- Laura Day. *Practical Intuition*. Villard Books, 1996.
- Joseph Campbell. *The Power of Myth with Bill Moyers*. Doubleday, 1988.
- Carol Lee Flinders. *Women Mystics*. HarperSanFrancisco, 1995
- Jean Houston. *A Mythic Life*. HarperSanFrancisco, 1996.
- Judith Orloff, M.D. *Second Sight*. Warner Books Inc. 1996.
- Brian L. Weiss, M.D. *Many Lives, Many Masters*. Fireside Simon & Schuster, 1988.
- Gary Zukav. *Seat of the Soul*.

Spirituality

- Anderson & Hopkins. *The Feminine Face of God: The Unfolding of the Sacred in Women*. Bantam, 1991.
- Mother M. Angelica with Christine Allison, *Mother Angelica's Answers, Not Promises*. Pocket Books, 1987.

- Babsie Baeasdell with Henry Libersat, *Refresh Your Life in the Spirit*. Charis, Servant Publications,1997.
- Fr. John Bertolucci. *On Fire with the Spirit*. Servant Books, 1984.
- Michael H. Brown. *Prayer of the Warrior*. Faith Publishing Company, 1993.
- Julia Cameron with Mark Bryan. *The Artist's Way*. Tarcher/Putnam, 1992.
- Anthony de Mello, *A Way to God*. Liguori/Triumph, 1931.
- Billy Graham. *Angels*. Word Publishing, 1995.
- Sue Monk Kidd, *God's Joyful Surprise*. HarperSanFransico, 1989.
- Sue Monk Kidd, *When the Heart Waits*. HarperSanFransico, 1990.
- Thomas Moore, *Care of the Soul & SoulMates*. HarperPerennial, 1992, 1994.
- M. Scott Peck, M.D. *The Road Less Traveled. The Road Less Traveled and Beyond. People of the Lie.* Touchstone, 1997.
- *Seeing with the Eyes of the Soul*, St Andrews Productions, 1998.
- G. Scott Sparrow, Ed.D. *I am with You Always*. Bantam, 1995.
- Marshall Vian Summers, *Wisdom from the Greater Community, Volumns 1 & 11*, 1993, 1996.
- Marianne Williamson. *A Return to Love*. Harper Perennial, 1993.

Miscellaneous

- James Redfield. *The Celestine Prophecy*. Warner Books.
- James Redfield. *The Tenth Insight*. Warner Books.
- James Redfield. *The Celestine Vision*. Warner Books.

What You Feel is Real – Dream Journal

To Order Your Dream Journal Go To:
www.transformationalleadersintl.com

TRANSFORMATIONAL LEADERS INTERNATIONAL

"Coaching for your Empowerment"

A Workbook Exercise

What You Feel is Real
The Wellness of Purpose

Level 1
The Divine Dive
Self Awareness Questions

Who are you?

_____

_____

_____

What excites you?

_____

_____

_____

What do you love to do?

_____

_____

_____

What do you want to do? (Not what someone else wants you to do)

_____

_____

_____

Is anything stopping you from what you like to do?

_____

_____

_____

Do you put others before yourself or your goals?

_____

_____

_____

Are there emotional barriers in your way?

_____

_____

_____

Are there physical barriers in your way?

_____

_____

_____

If you didn't have to worry about money, what would
you really do?

_____

_____

_____

What are your worst fears?

_____

_____

_____

Are you afraid of being judged?

_____

_____

_____

Level 2
The Divine Dive
Acceptance Actions – Take 3 days or more to process

- Take time to be with thoughts of, "Who you are"

- Feel, "Who you are"

- Visualize, "Who you are"

- Meditate on, "Who you are."

- Accept "Who you are"

Level 3
The Divine Dive
Questions of Purpose

What is most important to you?

_____

_____

_____

What has the most meaning to you?

_____

_____

_____

What do you really want to do with your life?

_____

_____

_____

What feels most comfortable?

_____
_____
_____

How do you see yourself?

_____
_____
_____

What images come to mind about what you're doing?

_____
_____
_____

Where do you feel it in your body?

_____
_____
_____

What does your heart say?

_____
_____
_____

What does your head say?

_____
_____
_____

Does the connection flow from your heart to head or from your head to my heart?

_____
_____
_____

Level 4
The Divine Dive
Truth Saying

FIRST – Say it to yourself, "Who you are"

SECOND – Say it out loud so you can hear, "Who you are"

THIRD – Look in the mirror and say it out loud, "Who you are"

FOURTH – Say it to someone else, "Who you are"

FIFTH – Ask someone to say it back to you, "Who you are"

SIXTH – Say it to yourself again, "Who you are"

Level 5
The Divine Dive
Focus on "Who You Are"

Label your core meaning of "Who you are" and other life roles in order of preference from the inside out.

Sample:

**The Divine Dive
Worksheet Exercise**

**Level 6
The Divine Dive
Your Statement**

I believe my purpose is

_____

_____

_____

_____

_____

_____

Level 7
The Divine Dive
Journaling

• Write your daily thoughts in a journal about "Who you are" and over time what you feel will become reality

The Divine Dive
Core Meaning Plan

Mission Statement of Purpose
(Same as your statement)

_____

_____

_____

_____

_____

_____

_____

_____

_____

Goals

	90 Days	Year 1	Year 5

1. _____

2. _____

3. _____

4. _____

5. _____

6. _____

7. _____

8. _____

9. _____

10. _____